CW00409877

ROUGH WATER
HANDLING

Doug Cooper

A PRACTICAL MANUAL

Published in Great Britain 2012 by Pesda Press

Tan y Coed Canol

Ceunant

Caernarfon

Gwynedd

LL55 4RN

© Copyright 2012 Doug Cooper

ISBN: 978-1-906095-34-5

The Author asserts the moral right to be identified as the author of this work.
All rights reserved. No part of this publication may be reproduced,
stored in a retrieval system, or transmitted, in any form or by
any means, electronic, mechanical, photocopying, recording or
otherwise, without the prior written permission of the Publisher.

Printed and bound in Poland. www.hussarbooks.pl

THE AUTHOR
Doug Cooper

Since writing *Sea Kayak Handling* (published by Pesda Press), Doug has continued to do what he enjoys doing most: paddling and coaching. Over the last few years this has taken him on expeditions to Alaska, Ladakh and Sardinia as well as plenty of coaching trips throughout the UK. Many of these expeditions have been in a sea kayak, but whitewater kayaking, mountaineering and skiing expeditions are also high on his agenda. When not coaching or away on expeditions, Doug can be found enjoying days off exploring Scotland's coastline or rivers or making fresh ski tracks when the winter snows arrive.

Doug works as Head of Paddlesport at Glenmore Lodge, Scotland's National Outdoor Centre. Here his love of helping others learn and improve is met every day, when he works as a BCU Level 5 Sea and Whitewater Coach, Level 4 Surf Coach and Mountain and Ski Instructor. A large proportion of his work is training and assessing paddlers working through the British Canoe Union's coaching and leadership qualifications system. As well as the delivery of these courses, Doug is also very involved in the development of the BCU courses as part of his role at Glenmore Lodge.

Doug's passion for the outdoors and sea kayaking is obvious from his work, lifestyle and publications (he also co-authored *Scottish Sea Kayaking*). This passion grows every year, as does the list of expeditions and places to explore. You will continue to see Doug enjoying the outdoors and exploring remote sections of coastline somewhere in the world well into the future.

ACKNOWLEDGEMENTS

It is always difficult to know where to start when it comes to offering thanks to those who have helped me. Over the years I have been lucky enough to paddle with many fantastic coaches and sea paddlers whom I have learnt from in many different ways. If I have ever been out on the sea with you, or chatted sea paddling over a beer in the bar, I have learnt from you and I thank you.

When it comes to getting an idea in my head into a book in your hand there are a few people who deserve specific mention. The biggest thanks go to my girlfriend, Lara Tipper. Pretty much all of the fantastic photographs in this book are down to her photographic expertise, patience and enthusiasm. Without her constant support, none of this would have been possible. In addition to Lara I also need to thank Olly Sanders for helping me out with a few photographs.

Throughout this book, you will see that a wide range of experienced coaches and paddlers have offered their own thoughts and words of wisdom. Their contributions have added greatly to the book and I appreciate their willingness to help me out.

Finally, I would of course like to thank all at Pesda Press who yet again have helped me out in every way I could ask for, producing another great book.

Photographs

All photos are by Lara Tipper and Doug Cooper except the Introduction and Chapter 1, 3, 4 and 9 heading photographs (which are by Olly Sanders), Chapter 5 heading photo (which is by Miki Miyashiro) and the good food and whisky photos in Chapter 8 which are by Dawn Horsburgh.

The main chapter photographs were taken at the following locations:

Chapter 2	North coast of Scotland
Chapter 3	Men of Mey Tidal Race, Pentland Firth; Falls of Lora
Chapter 4	Farr Beach (Sutherland); Grey Dogs Tidal Race (between Scarba and Lunga)
Chapter 5	Clachtoll (Sutherland)
Chapters 6–9	Various locations

INTRODUCTION

For the committed sea kayaker, the world's oceans offer constantly changing and challenging environments. Whether it is strong winds, rough seas, rolling swell, tidal races, surf beaches or open crossings, the ocean can be a very challenging place for the sea kayaker. In this dynamic environment the sea kayaker needs plenty of experience along with a high degree of skill not only to stay safe, but also to gain the highest rewards. For the sea kayaker who has the skills and experience to enjoy this environment, the challenges are endless. The pleasures that can be gained from these challenges, along with the places that can be explored, are out of this world.

The sea kayak that you are paddling has evolved through generations of experience and research, and nine times out of ten it will be the paddler who is the limiting factor when it comes to the boat performing in rough water. By getting to grips with the skills described in this book, putting in the practice and (most importantly) enjoying the learning opportunities, *Rough Water Handling* will hopefully open up a whole new world of exploration and challenge. I hope you enjoy the book and the opportunities it will provide for you, and I look forward to seeing you out there having fun on the rough stuff.

CONTENTS

USING THIS BOOK

The best way of ensuring that you can handle your sea kayak in rough water is to make sure you can edge, manoeuvre and handle your kayak with complete confidence and efficiency in calm water. You need to understand what techniques work best for you and your kayak in calm water, and why they work best.

To help you with the essential calmer water skills, ensure you have read, understood and practised the skills covered in *Sea Kayak Handling*. This is essential as, throughout this book, I will be referring to many of these skills and looking at how we adapt and use them in the various rough water environments.

Assumptions made

All of the skills in this book involve sea kayaking in potentially very challenging locations. This book in no way covers the huge amount of additional knowledge that is required to paddle safely at these locations; careful tidal planning and a good knowledge of navigation and weather are essential for all of the locations at which rough water handling takes place. The associated safety equipment and knowledge of how to use it is also required. Paddling as a group is advised at rough water locations; correspondingly, the knowledge and ability to look after each other as a group and perform rescues is essential. This book assumes that you have all this knowledge; if you feel you do not then there are other books to help with this (e.g. *Sea Kayak* by Gordon Brown or *Sea Kayak Navigation* by Franco Ferrero), but no book can replace training or coaching from competent or qualified sea kayakers.

Build up your experience gradually so that your theoretical knowledge is put to the test in manageable steps. The first time you go surfing, choose a gently shelving beach and wait for a day when the surf is small and the wind onshore. The first time you go to play in a tide race, go on neap tides. If you are not certain of the meaning of expressions such as 'onshore wind' or 'neap tides', read up on the theory in the above-mentioned books.

The final assumption I have made is that your kayak and equipment are suitable for the rough water environment. It is inevitable that you will get wetter out in the rough stuff and your boat will be challenged more (particularly in the wind). Good-quality sea kayak clothing is essential for your comfort, along with a sea kayak that is designed for exposed day and expedition paddling. Think back to the Connectivity section of the Foundation Skills chapter in *Sea Kayak Handling* and ensure that you are comfortably wearing your sea kayak!

Equipment and environmental considerations

Due to the nature of rough water environments, the variables are endless and different sea kayaks will be affected in different ways. Every paddler is different, whether in size, weight, flexibility, strength or confidence. Considering this, Rough Water Handling is in no way meant to be prescriptive or advocate that what is shown is the only way of doing it. All I have done is put together what has worked for me, as well as what has worked best for the majority of students I have coached over the years. This should give you a balanced view of ways to handle your sea kayak in rough water. Try what is shown in the book, then feel free to modify it a little to make it work best for you. Key equipment or environmental considerations are highlighted in separate information boxes throughout the book.

Learning and developing your skills

It is one thing flicking through a book and thinking that you can perform a skill; however, taking what is shown in a book and putting it to use for real it is quite another thing. The ideas and skills in the book are just to get you started on the right road to rough water sea kayak handling; it will be up to you to fully learn, understand and master these skills. Make sure that you set yourself appropriate goals that allow you to gradually build your skills. Start learning and practising the skills in a realistic environment, but one that is also forgiving and not too committing. This way, you can focus on learning the skill without the stress of thinking 'what happens if I blow it?' From this, build up gradually to those more committing environments where you need to know your skills will work.

Moving on from sea kayaking in calmer conditions requires the perfect blend of ingredients. To become skilled at paddling in rough conditions, I have adopted the multi-component model of skilful performance: technical, tactical, physiological and psychological or TTPP (as depicted).

A skilful performance needs to focus on these four main areas. Think of a skill you are already familiar with, and see if you can identify the separate TTPP parts within it. Consider the model when reading the book and revisit it when out paddling; it should help you to identify which 'ingredients' you need to focus on in your own paddling performance.

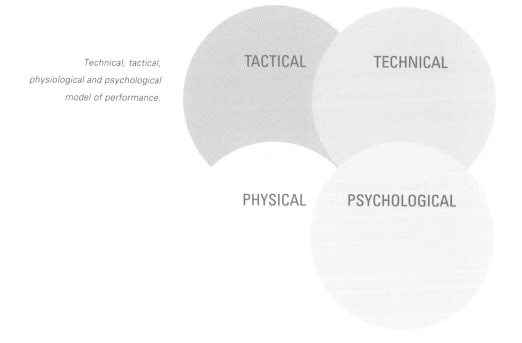

Technical, tactical, physiological and psychological model of performance.

TACTICAL   TECHNICAL

PHYSICAL   PSYCHOLOGICAL

By this stage, you will already have done a lot of learning to be able to paddle a sea kayak to a good standard. Everybody learns in different ways, and you will no doubt have your own preferred way. Before starting on some further learning and the associated practice, don't forget the following golden rules.

By following these simple rules you will get the most from the book and your practice sessions.

- Do not focus on too many skills at a time; otherwise, you will overload yourself as the learner.

- Always work on each skill on both sides (this is known as bilateral practice).

- Begin learning skills in an environment you feel comfortable in.

- As soon as you feel comfortable performing skills in one environment, change the environment to something more challenging.

- Practise your skills little and often so that you do not overtire each practice session; this should ensure the skills are being practised well.

- As well as changing sides and varying the environment when practising skills, also try varying the speed, range and power.

- Ask a friend to observe and pass feedback on what your skills look like in comparison to the pictures in the book.

- Ask a friend to take photographs or video footage of you performing your skills; you can then compare these to the book.

- After challenging your skills, take the time to reflect on what went well and what could be improved. Consider using the TTPP model above to help with this.

By following these simple golden rules you will get the most from your practice sessions and this book. Additional information boxes throughout the book also provide some coaching top tips either to help you practise or help you teach the skills yourself, as well as top tips from some of the world's leading sea paddlers and coaches.

As with learning all new skills, there is never any substitute to getting some quality coaching from a qualified instructor. You may want to consider this to speed up your journey to sea kayak mastery.

HIGH WIND PADDLING

There is no hiding from the fact that it is harder work and more awkward to keep control of your kayak on a windy day than on a calm day. With the appropriate skills, however, this does not need to be as hard as you may think. The key to high wind paddling is a good understanding of how your kayak works and what strokes combine with this best, as well as having the correct tactics to put it all together in the given wind. This chapter will explore all of this, looking at a variety of high wind situations that you may find yourself in as a sea kayaker.

Forward paddling

The most important part of forward paddling in the wind is the need to be as efficient as possible. Before we look specifically at paddling in high wind, you should revisit all those essential forward paddling skills. There are some additional tactics we can consider as well as some key points for us to remember in the main forward paddling styles. We consider a few tactics in the following.

High-angle forward paddling

If paddling against a strong wind this stroke will give you the most power to move forwards; fitness and technique will determine how long you can sustain this. If it can be maintained, this high-angle stroke will always be the most effective.

- Ensure the catch phase is maintained as far forward as is possible.

- Consider using a higher stroke rate (cadence) and shorter stroke length (finishing in front of hips) to help sustain the high-angle stroke for longer.

- Power transfer is key to maximising the forward stroke; remember foot pressure and rotation.

- Remember to sustain good posture to help with the above.

- Consider using a shorter paddle with a not-too-low feather angle if you have a choice (e.g. 208–212cm and 40–60° feather) when paddling in wind.

⇨ wind direction.
Top left: Paddling into the wind.
Top right: Paddling with the wind.

Bottom left: Paddling into the wind.
Bottom right: Paddling with the wind.

Low-angle forward paddling

For many this will be the most sustainable paddling style if going against the wind for any length of time. The lower angle and more sweeping nature of this stroke will feel more stable.

- Ensure that the blade is continually active (you feel pressure on it) to help this.

- If needing to suddenly accelerate for any reason, switching briefly from low-angle to high-angle paddling works well.

- Mixing the two styles while in the wind can also act as a way of resting different muscles when on a long paddle.

- Remember power transfer, rotation and good forward blade catch phase are all essential to maximise this stroke.

- Remember to sustain good posture to help with the above.

- A longer paddle with a not-too-low feather angle works well with this stroke (e.g. 214–220cm and 40–60° feather) in the wind.

There are some additional tactics we can also consider, as well as some key points for us to remember when paddling in different directions to the wind.

Paddling into the wind and waves

- The wind will 'lock' the bow of the boat in position, so on the low-angle paddling stroke you can extend the stroke a bit beyond the hips. This can help maintain momentum while setting up for the catch.

- Maintaining good rhythm, flow and technique is essential no matter what the waves are doing.

- Remember not to grip the paddle too tight; extend the fingers of your top hand when paddling to help avoid fatigue.

- Consider the timing of your strokes to prevent driving the bow into the waves and stalling the kayak. Try planting the blade on the fronts of the waves as they come towards you (as opposed to the backs of the waves) to help with this.

- Keep the skeg in the 'up' position.

COACH'S TOP TIP

Unfortunately, paddling in the wind takes as much grunt as skill! Providing you have the strength, a shorter paddle with a big blade is (for me) the best paddle to have. Normally when paddling in strong wind we are continually changing direction; feather is therefore less important as we won't always be paddling into head winds.

A shorter paddle will allow a more vertical stroke; this in turn will allow us to deliver more power to the blade.

In bigger and rougher seas remember the back of the blade is your best friend. When looking for that extra bit of stability at the end of a stroke, just leave the paddle in the water and the back of the blade will provide a little extra support until you choose to carry on paddling forwards. You will also be in an ideal position to low brace if you need to.

Blade area is important; for example, when paddling downwind in moderate conditions, it takes me one powerful stroke to get on the front of a wave with a $750cm^2$ blade, two with a $700cm^2$ and three with a $650cm^2$. Unfortunately, bigger blades in the wind can cause strains and tendon problems, so it will depend on your strength and stamina. By experimenting with this and the right paddle length you will find the best solution for you.

Nigel Dennis

Nigel circumnavigated Great Britain in 1980 and has since been on numerous expeditions which include Antarctica, Cape Horn, Easter Island, South Georgia and a good deal more. He started designing and building kayaks back in 1995 and has recently purchased Lendal paddles. To find out more, visit the *www.seakayakinguk.com* and *www.lendal.com* websites.

Paddling with the wind and waves

- Ensure you have your skeg down and/or the kayak trimmed slightly rear-heavy so that the kayak tracks efficiently.

- If any correction strokes are needed for steering, try and use the stern draw as opposed to a stern rudder as this will slow the kayak down less.

- Do not use forward sweep strokes to try to turn as the kayak will have overtaken the blade before any real power is generated in the stroke, rendering it useless.

- Time the forward strokes to try to catch any waves to help generate forward speed (see the 'Surfing' chapter).

- As waves pick up the kayak, try moving your upper body forwards a little to help pick up the wave and generate extra speed.

- If stability becomes an issue, use low-angle forward paddling as the more sweeping nature will increase stability.

- If stability is an issue and you need to control the kayak at all, use the braced stern rudder.

Paddling across wind and waves

- It is fundamental here to ensure that the kayak is tracking straight so that all power can go into moving the kayak forwards and not correcting direction.

- The most efficient way to obtain good tracking is through use of the skeg and/or trim; if this does not work there are alternatives. See the chapter on 'Travelling in a straight line' in *Sea Kayak Handling* to help with this.

- Keeping relaxed at the hips is vital; this allows the kayak to stay running straight and the wave to roll under you.

- For stability and to keep power in the forward paddling, good posture needs to be maintained with relaxed hips.

- Try and time the strokes so that the blade is in constant contact with the water; it should feel active all the way through the stroke.

Ferry glide angle being used for paddling across the wind.
⇨ *wind direction.*
➡ *ground track*

- To get to where you need to be, you will most probably be ferry gliding against the wind (see the 'Moving water' chapter). Use transits to help with the ferry glide angle.

TOP TIPS

To be able to tactically handle a sea kayak in high winds, it is essential to understand how the wind affects the kayak you are paddling and why. For any manoeuvre, ensure that the tactics of the turn and techniques of the chosen stroke work with the kayak and the wind to make it as easy as possible.

With the kayak side-on to the wind and with no skeg, paddle forwards and backwards to see what direction the kayak naturally wants to turn. Then sit still and do nothing and see which way the kayak moves or wants to turn.

You may well find that when going forwards the bow of the boat is locked in the water and the stern blows downwind; when going backwards the stern locks and the bow blows downwind faster than when the stern blows downwind. When sat doing nothing, the whole kayak will blow sideways and the bow will most probably blow downwind slightly faster than the stern. All the following tactics and techniques of the manoeuvres are based on these facts. All kayaks will perform slightly differently and the way they are packed will have an effect. If your kayak reacts differently to what is described above, take this into consideration in the manoeuvring described in this chapter.

Turning from a static start

You may have stopped for a rest or have stalled your kayak while trying to turn on the move. Whatever the reason, trying to turn a sea kayak in strong winds from a static start can be very challenging. Turning can be made easier by considering the tactics of which way to best turn the kayak in relation to the wind and by using the appropriate strokes. The key point is to get the kayak moving; combined with the effect of the wind, this will generally allow a turn to start naturally.

Downwind turning

From a static position with a side wind, it is usually easier to turn the bow of the kayak downwind as opposed to upwind. This is due to the fact that the bow of the kayak will generally have more 'windage' than the stern (i.e. since more of the bow will be clear of the water than the stern, it

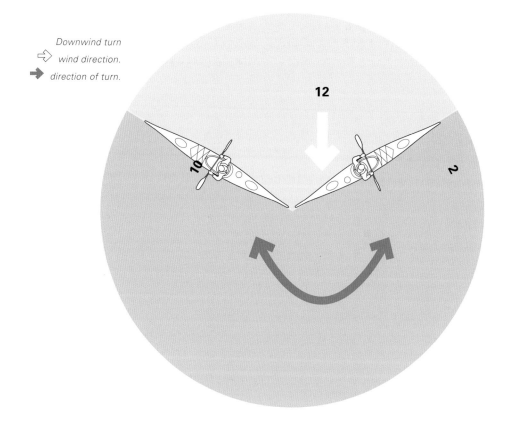

Downwind turn
⇨ wind direction.
➡ direction of turn.

will be affected by the wind more) and we can use this to good effect to help us turn. I would therefore recommend using the following turn to move the kayak from a static start; I would also use this method when wanting to move the bow of the kayak through any position highlighted in the diagram.

The downwind turn described is a bit like doing a reverse three-point turn. I have referred to the technique as the 'reverse braced handbrake turn' in Sea Kayak Handling and it can also be referred to as the 'high wind turn'. This downwind turn starting from a static position is carried out as follows.

1 + **2**   Paddle the kayak backwards and initiate the turn.

SKEG UP

- Start the kayak moving backwards and the bow will naturally start to move downwind.

- Moving the body back a little to stern trim will assist the above.

- By moving the kayak in reverse, it 'locks' the stern in the water and allows the bow to blow downwind easier; the reverse sweep helps the process.

- Initiate the turn with a reverse sweep to move the stern of the kayak up into the wind.

- To maximise the power in the reverse sweep, ensure that at the start of the stroke the blade is moved powerfully away from the side of the kayak (like a pry stroke or a sideways thruster on a ferry).

- Apply as much edge and power as you feel comfortable with (the more the better).

- Have the skeg up to help with the turn.

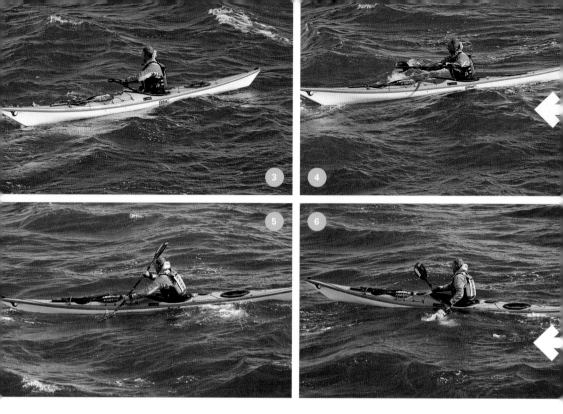

3 + 4 Use additional reverse sweep strokes while maintaining backwards momentum.

- Continue with additional reverse sweep strokes as required to move the bow into a downwind position.

- To get more power out of the reverse sweep, lift through your knees towards your paddle blade.

- To help with stability on the edge, angle the back of the blade so it offers support.

- Ensure that backwards momentum is maintained.

- Using these reverse sweep strokes and the wind, the kayak should be in a downwind position. If this is enough of a turn you are good to go, if not continue the stroke as shown in the following two photos.

5 + 6 Using the high brace sweeping stroke to continue the turn.

- Once the bow of the kayak is pointing downwind, it is best to use the following to continue the turn as required.

- Ensure the kayak has backwards momentum.

- Place the non-reverse sweeping blade in a high braced blade position as far forwards as can comfortably be reached on the opposite side to the reverse sweep stroke.

- At the same time, change edge so that the kayak is edged as much as is possible towards the high braced blade.

- The body should be facing in the turning direction.

- Ensure the front face of the braced blade is offering support by pulling down on it; angle the top edge of the blade up slightly so that it does not dive in the water.

- Move the braced paddle through the water from the bow of the kayak in an arc to about level with the hips.

- Use core rotation to move the braced paddle and push on the down-edge lower foot for power transfer.

- Use the waves to assist by trying to time the high braced turn when the kayak is at the top of a wave. This frees up the bow and stern, thus making the turn easier.

- At this stage the kayak will have come to a stop. If you need to turn the kayak further, read on.

7 + 8 With the kayak now static, add a reverse sweep to finish the turn if required.

- If you are requiring a little bit more out of the turn, do another reverse sweep on the opposite side to the high brace turn just carried out.

- At this stage you will most likely be trying to turn the bow of the kayak up into the wind, so this will have limited effect.

- If further turning is needed, consider the following upwind turning method.

Upwind turning

Starting from static the bow of the kayak catches more wind, therefore the upwind turn will inevitably be harder. Tactically, it makes sense to move the stern of the kayak through the wind wherever possible. There are however times when we need to turn our kayak upwind when static, and this can be carried out as follows.

1 + 2   Get the kayak moving forwards and use sweep strokes to start the turn.

SKEG UP

- To start this turn it is best to get some forward speed on the kayak, this will 'lock' the bow of the kayak and allow the stern to be blown downwind.

- To help 'lock' the bow of the kayak, move your upper body forwards to increase the weight at the bow of the kayak and get help from this trim.

- Initiate a forward sweep stroke.

- Ensure good forward speed is maintained with the sweep strokes.

- Remember to edge towards the blade and gain support from it as much as is comfortable.

- Have the skeg in the 'up' position.

3 + **4**   Using trim and powerful sweep strokes on the move to continue the turn.

- Focus on getting as much power into the forward sweep as possible.

- To maximise the power in the forward sweep, ensure that at the start of the stroke the blade is moved powerfully away from the side of the kayak (like a pry stroke or a sideways thruster on a ferry).

- Remember the power transfer through the foot nearest the blade.

- Look where you are turning to help engage the core muscles.

- Finish the forward sweep as far back as allows you to maintain an edge and feel stable in the conditions.

- Finishing the sweep stroke towards the rear (or even using a stern draw) will help move the stern downwind.

- If there is enough space keep the kayak moving forwards and repeat the sweep strokes, keeping the body weight forwards to bow trim the kayak.

- If these bow-trimmed sweep strokes on the move are not enough to turn the kayak upwind, or there is not enough space to keep the kayak moving, continue with the following.

5 + **6**   Using reverse sweeps on the top of a wave to continue the turn with the kayak static.

- As soon as a forward sweep is finished, change edge to initiate a reverse sweep.

- The reverse sweep should be initiated as far back as is stable.

- Gain support from the reverse sweep to hold as much of an edge as is possible.

- Apply as much power to the reverse sweep as you can.

- Remember to drive the blade away from the boat at the start of the stroke.

- Use good power transfer by lifting your knees towards the paddle blade and applying pressure on feet to help with this.

- Finish the reverse sweep as far forward as is possible.

- Try to initiate the reverse sweep at the top of a wave to help the turn; this works because the bow and stern are less locked in the water.

Continuing the static turn with a forward sweep stroke

- If this has not turned the kayak enough upwind, then repeat the process by initiating another forward sweep stroke.

Turning on the move: paddling downwind

In high winds this is the easiest direction of travel in which to turn a kayak. With the wind blowing the paddler along, there is plenty of speed to help with the turn. The key thing to be aware of in all the following turns is that, as the kayak is moving, the bow of the boat will be 'locked' tight in the water as it cuts through. With this in mind, all turning strokes work best by focusing on turning the 'looser' stern of the kayak.

TOP TIPS

Trim has a huge effect on the sea kayak when paddling in the wind. You can adjust the trim of the kayak by moving your upper body forwards or backwards while paddling. Try paddling forwards side-on to the wind. While maintaining the forward stroke move your body as far forward as is comfortable; notice the effect and how the kayak will turn more into the wind. Try this again but this time move your body as far back as is comfortable while paddling. Notice how this will slow the upwind turning of the kayak, or even make the kayak start to turn downwind. Experiment with the above while increasing the speed of paddling. Often the faster you paddle the quicker the kayak will move upwind; the slower you paddle the less it will turn upwind. Knowledge of the effect of speed and trim can be used to help turn the kayak in the wind.

Left: rear trim. Right: forward trim.

Any turning strokes that are attempted towards the front of the kayak are relatively ineffective. This is because the kayak is travelling fast and it will have overtaken the blade before any power can be gained from it. (Remember the principle with all strokes that the blade is fixed in the water and the kayak is moving past it.)

With these main tactical considerations, there are three effective strokes for turning when paddling downwind as described in the following.

Stern rudder

The stern rudder can be used to keep the kayak tracking in a straight line and prevent the need to turn, as well as allowing some turning. The stern rudder is the most efficient method of keeping directional control of the kayak in a following wind. It does require a good awareness of what is happening to the boat, so it can be used efficiently as prevention as opposed to cure. It also takes confidence to use in rougher conditions due to the amount of rotation required.

Right: High-angle stern rudder to maintain direction.

Top: Skeg position for travelling straight downwind.

Bottom: Skeg position if turning is required.

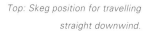
SKEG DOWN

- The high-angle stern rudder has greatest effect.

- It can be used while the skeg is down to maintain direction.

- If needing to alter direction, then the skeg can be raised.

- At speed, using the edge and feathering the blade works best for directional control and turning.

- Good rotation must be used so that the blade does not have any braking effect.

SKEG UP

- The blade is best placed as far back and as deep as is comfortable, as well as being close to the side of the kayak.

If I was very tired and happy to move at a reasonable speed for the least effort, I would have my skeg down when travelling in a following wind and sea. However, most of the time I don't do this; although it requires more skill and effort, you can travel much faster and surf more waves without the drag caused by the skeg.

You do have to be more 'switched on' however; constantly alter your trim with your body weight, continually alter the pressure on your feet, switch from forward paddling to stern rudders and vary the amount of pressure on the blade performing the rudder.

It's demanding, but exhilarating and rewarding. With two other paddlers I once travelled in this fashion for 40NM in a 12 foot following sea and a Force 6 wind. Had we been going any faster, we'd have got there before we started!

Franco Ferrero

Franco is a keen sea paddler whose latest variation on the theme is to combine sailing with kayaking by using three-piece kayaks. He is also the owner of Pesda Press, the author of *Sea Kayak Navigation* and a BCU Level 5 Coach.

Bracing stern rudder

The best feature of the bracing stern rudder is that in the roughest of seas it offers support, stability, directional control and turning. With this in mind, it quickly becomes the default setting when enjoying those following big seas or squally high winds out in the rough stuff. The disadvantage of this stroke is that it will have a braking effect; for downwind turning this is not usually a problem, however.

Right: The bracing stern rudder in action.

Below: Skeg position.

SKEG DOWN

- With the kayak moving, half rotate the upper body.

- Place the blade in a low braced position just behind the hips, ensuring the back of the braced blade is providing support by gently pushing down on it and having it out from the kayak.

- Angle the blade slightly up at its front edge so it does not dive in the water.

- Edge the kayak slightly towards the low braced blade, keeping constant pressure on the up-edge knee and feet.

- By applying gentle pressure, the rudder can be used to stop the kayak turning and provide support. In the photo the paddler is using the braced stern rudder to stop the kayak turning right.

- The skeg can be left in the 'down' position for this manoeuvre.

1 + 2   Using the bracing stern rudder to turn the kayak by moving the paddle out from the kayak.

- By increasing the pressure and increasing the edge towards the rudder, you can increase the turning effect if required.

SKEG UP

- To assist the turning, it is best to move the skeg into the 'up' position.

- If further turning is required, move the blade out from the kayak to become level with the hips in a braced position.

- To maximise power transfer during this braced turning, think about moving the up-edge knee towards the bracing paddle with the core muscles engaged.

- To help with this part of the turn, try to time it as the kayak is positioned at the top of a wave if possible.

- The kayak should be easily turned so that it is pointing across the wind.

- At this stage, the kayak will be static in the water and an upwind turn (as already described) can be used if further turning is required.

Stern draw

The main tactical advantage of the stern draw is that it turns the kayak without too much of a slowing effect. When paddling downwind, trying to avoid losing speed and when stability is not an issue, this is a great stroke to use.

1 + 2 Using the stern draw to turn the kayak.

SKEG UP

- The stern draw can be initiated at the end of a forward paddling stroke as part of the keyhole stroke, or used repeatedly on its own.

- Keep looking in the direction of travel.

- Edge the kayak towards the paddle as much as feels comfortable in the conditions; only a small amount of edge is needed to have a good effect.

- Pull the blade in towards the stern of the kayak to start the turn.

- Do this by rotating the body as well as pushing the front hand at chest height across the body out over the water and pulling with the rear hand to draw the stern of the kayak towards the blade.

- This push/pull method of a draw (as opposed to the fully rotating method of stern sweep stroke) should be more stable in rougher conditions.

- Having the skeg up will help the turn, but is not essential.

3 + 4 + 5   Linking additional stern draws using a skimming blade in the recovery phase.

- To link more than one stern draw, remove the blade before it touches the side of the kayak.

- Repeat the stern draw as many times as is required.

- Try to maintain the kayak on edge while moving the blade to start a new stern draw.

- To help maintain the kayak on a balanced edge, the blade can be skimmed across the surface in an emergency stabiliser position when moving it out to the new stroke initiation.

- Use the tops of any waves to assist the turn.

COACH'S TOP TIP

Turning in high winds is quite possibly one of the most important things to master when sea kayaking. A strong offshore wind will affect the kayak more than an onshore wind of a similar strength, since there are little or no waves to hide behind.

The ability to commit to the lean or edge phase of the stroke sequence is key; by keeping your kayak off balance for longer you are shortening the waterline length and enabling a faster turn. Always use a climbing blade angle to assist with this in the leaning phase and, when proficient, move onto a more powerful upright or even slightly diving blade angle to power your way through the sequence. Even though the kayak is off balance, whether on the downwind or upwind side, there will be enough support from the active blade to allow full commitment of your body weight to the paddle. As soon as the active blade starts to power-up, use your core muscles to increase the potency of the turn. Because you are already sitting in a strong dynamic position with good connections between you and the kayak, all of your leg and back muscles are ready to add power at the appropriate time.

By developing your ability to turn the kayak in a strong wind, you are greatly improving your likelihood of getting to the shore quickly and safely.

Gordon Brown

Gordon has been sea kayaking for 39 years and has spent much of that time coaching others. He set up Skyak Adventures on the Isle of Skye where he paddles most days. He produced the first sea kayak rescue video *Over... and Out* in 1993 and since then has written the chapter on sea kayaking for the current BCU *Canoe and Kayak Handbook* (Pesda Press) as well as the hugely successful *Sea Kayak* (Pesda Press). More recent times have seen the release of the popular Sea Kayak with Gordon Brown DVD series (Sunart Media). For more information on Gordon and Skyak Adventures visit *www.skyakadventures.com* and *www.seakayakwithgordonbrown.com*.

Turning on the move: paddling upwind

When paddling upwind, the bow of the boat will be 'locked' in position. To turn the kayak, the tactics are therefore to make maximum use of the waves and wind to help make this turn as easy as possible. That said, an element of strength will definitely help. If this is still not working, there is the golden 'high wind turn' available to us!

Forward sweep turn

In the majority of conditions this will be the best turn to use; however, it does take good timing and the ability to perform a forward sweep stroke on the move with maximum power and efficiency.

 Initiating the sweep stroke so the turn happens on the top of the wave.

SKEG UP

- The timing of this stroke is critical; start the sweep stroke on the face of an oncoming wave.

- Initiate the stroke as far forward as possible with as much edge towards the paddle as is comfortable.

- With the stroke initiated on the wave face, the power of the sweep should be transferred when the bow of the kayak is up in the air on top of the wave.

- With the bow in the air it is 'unlocked' from the water and is free to catch more wind; this all helps the turn.

- Remember to look in the direction of the turn and transfer power through the foot nearest the blade.

- To maximise the power in the forward sweep, ensure that at the start of the stroke the blade is moved powerfully away from the side of the kayak (like a pry stroke or a sideways thruster on a ferry).

- Finish the sweep stroke when it is level with the hips; this maximises turning while ensuring stability.

- The skeg needs to be in the 'up' position to help with the turn.

3 Using additional sweep strokes to continue the turn.

- If further turning is required to get side-on to the waves and wind, repeat the sweep stroke process while remembering the timing with the waves.

- To help with stability, skim the back of the blade across the water so it is available as an emergency stabiliser when moving it back to the front of the kayak to initiate the next sweep stroke.

- Using these sweep strokes, enough of a turning effect may be achieved.

- If more turning is required, consider using the following bracing turn.

4 + 5 + 6   Using the braced 'handbrake' turn to finish turning the kayak.

- When finishing a sweep stroke once across the waves, apply a braced handbrake turn.

- To get a tighter turn, move the bracing blade from just behind the hip to near the knees.

- To maximise the power transfer in this, think about moving the up-edge knee towards the paddle blade.

- Make use of any waves to help with the braced handbrake turn where possible.

- Finish the turn with a further sweep stroke if required.

- By putting the skeg in the 'down' position once the bow of the kayak is downwind, it will help with the turn.

Reverse braced handbrake turn

The sweep turn works well; however, there will come a time when the wind is so strong that it will be physically difficult (or even impossible) to unlock the bow of the kayak to start the turn. When this becomes the case, it is time to think tactically and start working with the wind and the kayak as opposed to against them. At this stage, going backwards is the answer! The fact that a turn is required will mean that moving forwards is no longer the priority; this allows a reverse turn to become an option. The reverse turn allows the paddler to go with the wind; this is easier and also has the advantage of going backwards, therefore locking the stern as opposed to the bow. All of this will make the turn surprisingly easy, even in the strongest of winds. This turn quickly becomes the 'get-out-of-jail-free' turn when all else fails to get the bow turned off the wind, hence its other name: the high wind turn.

- **1** Getting the kayak moving backwards by reverse paddling.

- To get the turn started, paddle backwards using the oncoming waves to assist in getting some speed up.

- Ensure that the skeg is in the 'up' position.

- Once moving, 'feel' what way the boat naturally wants to turn; the waves and wind will dictate this.

- **2** + **3** Using reverse sweep strokes to help the kayak turn across the wind.

- Once the boat starts to turn in a certain direction, use reverse sweep strokes to help the turn.

- Remember to start these strokes as far back as is comfortable and edge towards the paddle.

- Gain support from the blade, apply good power and finish the stroke when it is about level with the knees.

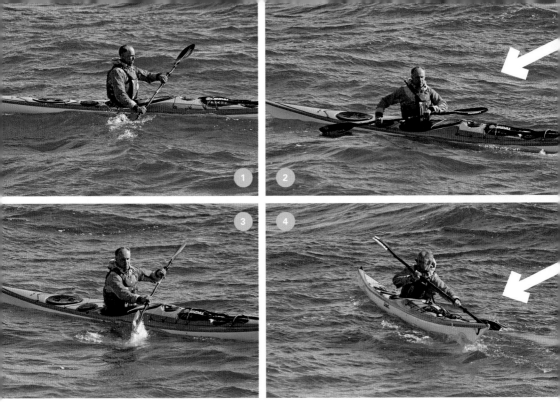

- By using the momentum of the waves and wind along with sweep strokes, the kayak should easily turn so the bow is well off the wind (perhaps to nearly 90°).

- Use linked reverse sweep strokes to get it to this position.

- Initiating the reverse handbrake turn with the blade in a high brace position as far as is comfortable.

- While the kayak still has backwards momentum, place the paddle in a high braced blade position as far forward as can comfortably be reached on the opposite side to the reverse sweep stroke.

- When placing the braced blade, ensure the body is rotated and you are looking in the direction of the turn.

- At the same time as this, change edge so that the kayak is edged as much as is possible towards the high braced blade, which should offer plenty of support.

- The kayak will slow down and start turning around the braced blade.

5 Moving the blade in an arc to become level with the hips, turning the kayak.

● To increase the turn, move the braced paddle through the water from the front of the kayak in an arc to about level with the hips.

● Use core rotation to move the braced paddle by looking in the direction of the turn; push on the down-edge lower foot for power transfer.

● As the kayak comes to a stop, flatten the edge and remove the braced blade from the water.

6 + **7** Using additional sweep strokes to continue the turn.

● If the sea kayak has not turned far enough, you will be able to use an additional sweep stroke to finish.

● Consider putting the skeg down at this stage to help move/maintain the bow downwind when paddling off.

SKEG DOWN

EQUIPMENT CONSIDERATIONS

How the sea kayak is set up and how it is affected by the wind has a huge outcome on all paddling in the wind. To have the kayak set up so that it turns slightly upwind when paddled forwards in a side wind is very useful; this gives the paddler the ability to use this to assist turning. Set the kayak up so that it is trimmed for this to happen; this can be done by how it is loaded or by adjusting the seat position. With the kayak set up like this, the paddler can use the skeg to cancel out the effect of the wind or, indeed, by having the skeg fully down to turn the kayak downwind. This clearly gives the paddler ultimate control of how the kayak performs in the wind, which can then be used to help with high wind manoeuvres.

If the kayak does not have a skeg, it will generally be trimmed so it is affected as little as possible by the wind. This can however lead to the kayak becoming more 'locked' by the wind, making the manoeuvring very difficult.

Turning on the move: paddling with a side wind

When the wind and waves are coming from the side, it becomes essential to know how the kayak reacts to the wind. In particular, is it essential to know how it naturally turns due to wind effect alone. The majority of appropriately trimmed sea kayaks will weathercock slightly, i.e. move bow to wind. The following methods of turning take this fact into consideration.

Turning upwind

When a kayak's bow moves into the wind it is because it is locked in the water and the wind is blowing the stern downwind. Knowing this allows us to think tactically and use the stern draw to help move the stern downwind quicker, as opposed to a forward sweep stroke that would need a lot of power to move the locked bow of the kayak upwind. Both would have the same effect of turning the kayak upwind; however, one can be more efficient than the other. For this reason I would generally choose the stern draw as my preferred way of turning a sea kayak upwind in this situation.

1   Stern draw initiation with good kayak speed and forward trim to help start the turn.

SKEG UP

●   Paddle the kayak forwards with good speed (the faster the kayak is moving, the more locked the bow becomes) and move your body weight forward to anchor the bow further.

●   Initiate the stern draw on the downwind side of the kayak.

●   Ensure the skeg is in the 'up' position so that the stern is free to be blown and moved downwind.

●   Place the stern draw as far back and out from the kayak as is comfortable.

- Good rotation with both hands out over the water will help with this, while looking in the direction of travel.

- Edge towards the stern draw as much as is possible; however, it takes very little edge to help the turn.

2 + 3 The power phase of the stern draw and use of a skimming blade to help maintain balance when setting up for another stroke.

- Move the blade towards the stern of the kayak to help draw it downwind.

- Having the blade face slightly angled towards the kayak will give some support.

- Use the push/pull technique for the draw to prevent over-rotating (this helps with stability).

- To help maintain the kayak on a balanced edge while performing a second stern draw, the blade can be skimmed across the surface in an emergency stabiliser position when moving it out to the new stroke initiation.

4 + 5 Linking stern draws to continue the turn.

- Repeat the stern draws as many times as is required to turn the kayak upwind.

Turning downwind

Turning the kayak downwind is often going to be a little harder as it is usually working against what the kayak wants to do naturally. With this considered, a number of different strokes may well be required depending on how far downwind the bow of the kayak needs to be moved. Initiate the turn by timing it with the waves and using efficient sweep strokes. To complete the stroke, a braced handbrake turn may be needed. If all else fails, don't forget the static downwind turn using the reverse braced handbrake turn; this uses far less power, works with the wind and may save time in high winds.

SKEG DOWN

1 Sweep stroke initiation, using slower kayak speed and rear trim to help start the turn.

● Stop paddling the kayak so it starts to slow down; the slower the kayak, the less locked-in is the bow.

● Move your body weight back as far as is comfortable; this stern trims the kayak thus helping the bow to blow downwind.

● Initiate a forward sweep stroke on the upwind side.

● Reach well forward and edge towards the blade.

● To maximise the power in the forward sweep, ensure that at the start of the stroke the blade is moved powerfully away from the side of the kayak.

● Having the skeg fully down will help the bow of the kayak blow downwind.

2 Sweep stroke power phase, finishing level with the hips.

● Time the power part of the stroke to coincide with the top of a wave if possible; this will help with the turning of the kayak.

● To maximise the power in the sweep, remember to look where the kayak is turning and keep the blade fully submerged throughout the stroke.

- Apply plenty of power transfer by pushing on the foot nearest the blade.

- Finish the sweep stroke when the blade is about level with the hips, as this will maximise power and maintain stability.

3 + **4** + **5**   Linking sweep strokes to continue the turn and using a skimming blade to help maintain balance when setting up for another stroke.

- To turn the kayak so that it faces further downwind, continue with the sweep strokes.

- To help with stability, skim the back of the blade across the water so it is available as an emergency stabiliser when moving it back to the front of the kayak to initiate the next sweep stroke.

- Maintain a comfortable edge on the kayak at all times, and remember maximum power transfer on further sweep strokes.

6 + 7   Using the braced handbrake to finish the turn, making use of any waves.

- Once the kayak is starting to face downwind, if further turning is required a braced handbrake turn can be applied.

- Start the braced handbrake turn when finishing a sweep stroke.

- This works best if carried out when the kayak is on top of a wave that is coming from the side.

- Use this wave to help with the braced handbrake turn so that the kayak almost surfs down the wave to finish the turn.

- For a tighter turn, move the bracing blade from just behind the hip to near the knees.

- To maximise the power transfer, move both knees towards the paddle blade.

- In kayak surfing, this is similar to a top pivot turn!

- Maintain the downwind position by ensuring the skeg is in the 'down' position once the bow of the kayak is downwind.

EQUIPMENT CONSIDERATIONS

For the side wind turns, if the kayak does not naturally move bow to wind then the turns described may not be the most efficient. To help this, consider trimming the kayak so that it does go slightly bow to wind.

If this is not possible then different tactics may be required. If the kayak moves naturally bow downwind, then the sweep strokes described will work easier for downwind turning. However, it may work better with powerful forward sweep strokes using the waves for the upwind turn. If the kayak is neutral in the wind then powerful sweep strokes will be required. In both instances, experiment with what works best for you and also consider the reverse turns.

TOP TIPS

It is clear that all aspects of the Technical, Tactical, Physiological and Psychological model are required to manoeuvre a kayak well in the wind. Here are some examples of where some key aspects of this chapter fit into the model. Consider these and add more to the lists depending on the exact turn you are interested in. You can then use them as a way of analysing what areas you will benefit most from practising. Consider this when looking at the rest of the chapters in the book.

TACTICAL

Direction to turn bow in relation to wind.

When to start turn in relation to wave.

When to use the skeg.

Bow turns or stern turns?

TECHNICAL

Where to initiate the stroke.

Where to finish the stroke.

How to transfer power.

How to maintain edge.

PHYSICAL

Core strength.

Flexibility.

Stamina.

Hydration.

Energy levels.

PSYCHOLOGICAL

Relaxed in environment.

Confident of outcome.

Appropriate arousal.

Appropriate focus.

MOVING WATER

As the sea constantly flows around the world's coastlines, getting squeezed between landmasses or forced around headlands, it speeds up. This flow of water may be barely noticeable but, at many locations, it can form mighty tidal races and overfalls that are more akin to a raging river than the sea. A committed sea paddler exploring these coastlines will inevitably have to negotiate some of these tidal races and overfalls. Indeed, others will actively seek out these venues to challenge themselves.

To enjoy these environments the ability to paddle a kayak efficiently in moving water is essential; this chapter will look at the range of skills at our disposal to do this. Although this chapter is focused on moving water it should be noted that, when 'ferry gliding' in wind or 'breaking in' to strong wind and waves, the skills being described are very transferable.

PSYCHOLOGICAL FACTORS

Confidence only comes with habituation and the knowledge that you have the skills to cope. Paddling through a tidal race that has 'kicked up' bigger than expected can be a terrifying experience for those who have little experience of overfalls. Time spent playing in manageable conditions and building up your skills and experience is a good investment.

outer tide race

eddy

eddy line

downstream 'V'

eddy

breaking waves

breaking waves

A tidal race where the moving water features are clearly seen.

Manoeuvring in the flow

For most kayakers, the first experience of a tidal race is just paddling into one and then through it. They will paddle round a headland, paddle through the tidal race and continue on the journey. If the journey is the objective, they may well see no need to break in or break out of the flow; they might need to manoeuvre the kayak while in the flow, however. Paddlers who enjoy playing in the tidal races need to get out to a wave or line up for a break-out, so for them the need to be able to change direction efficiently is more obvious.

Either way, having the confidence, knowledge and skills to move around efficiently in a tidal race is essential; we cover these in the start of this chapter. To help with this, understanding how a tidal race works and how the water moves is important. Look at the above image and identify the areas of slacker water (called eddies), the waves or broken water and then the smoother downstream 'V's of flowing water.

Paddling with the flow

For those new to paddling in moving water and tidal races, start to get to grips with the environment by choosing a venue that allows you to paddle from calmer water through a tidal race and then back to calmer water; this type of location is perfect for gaining confidence in the rough stuff. Time should be spent doing this as well as gaining the confidence and ability to manoeuvre in the tidal race; this is what is required to survive and, more importantly, enjoy any tidal race.

Top left: Look for the best line to paddle.

Top right: Stay relaxed with an active paddle

- Keeping relaxed is key to performing in a tidal race (see the 'Psychological considerations' chapter).

- Focus on keeping loose at the hips to allow the boat to move separately from the upper body; this allows the waves to pass under the boat and stability to be maintained.

- Keep an 'active paddle' all the time (feeling constant pressure on the blade) to help stability.

- Maintain a speed that is faster or slower than the flow; this way the boat is controlled by the paddler rather than the flow.

- Keep looking well ahead, focusing on where the kayak is going.

- Look for the best line to paddle through the waves.

- Maintain a constant forward paddling stroke; a higher angle gives power if needed. If going with the flow this may not be needed however and a lower angle can give extra stability.

- Time the strokes so that the blade makes constant contact with the water.

- Keep a forward posture, particularly when going through waves as this increases stability.

- If going over bigger waves try to reach forwards to plant the paddle stroke over the wave.

Paddling across the flow

There are two main ways to get across the flow: one that maintains the position of the kayak within the flow and one that allows the kayak to be moved with the flow. Maintaining position within the flow is known as ferry gliding and is covered later in the chapter. Allowing the kayak to be moved with the flow is far easier physically, so if journeying through a tidal race and maintaining position is not needed then use this. From a tactical point of view, if you know that you will need to move across the flow at some time, plan to move across early when you can go with the flow to save energy (as opposed to leaving it later and having to try to ferry glide).

➡ *direction of flow*

1 Staying relaxed while paddling across the flow.

- Keep relaxed and loose at the hips to help stability.

- A slight downstream edge (i.e. raise the upstream knee and look downstream) will help with stability.

- Keep an active paddle as well as constant forward paddle strokes.

- Keep visual awareness of your position in the tidal race to know how fast to paddle. Aim to paddle at a relaxed speed.

- Time the strokes so that the blade is fully in the water.

2 Bracing onto a breaking wave from the side.

- If steeper waves come from the side, edge towards the wave (i.e. raise the knee on the opposite side to which the wave is approaching).

- Keep a forward body posture for stability.

- Keep relaxed at the hips.

- If stability is a concern use a low brace for support, aiming to place the low brace on top of the wave.

- Continue forward paddling when the wave has passed under the kayak.

Wide turns in the flow

When out in the flow it is normal that a change of direction may be needed, for example to avoid a potential hazard or to start lining up the kayak for a break-out. The first thing is to consider is tactics: how tight does the turn need to be and how much time is available? If there is plenty of time forward speed can be maintained and the turn does not need to be too tight, as described in the following.

1 + 2 Using the forward sweep to turn in the flow.

- The forward sweep turn gives plenty of power while maintaining speed.

- Focus on power transfer through the body and foot in the first half of the sweep.

- Use as much edge as is comfortable to help the turn.

- Use a skimming recovery stroke between linked sweeps to help with stability.

- Time the turn to use the top of a wave to help whenever possible. Start the sweep as you are going up a wave face to get maximum power on the blade; the turn then happens on top of the wave.

- Look for any changes of speed in the water (micro eddies/boils in the flow) to help with the turn.

- Time the sweep stroke to coincide with entering such water to help with the turn.

- If it is windy, refer to the 'High-wind paddling' chapter to see how best to use the wind to help the turns.

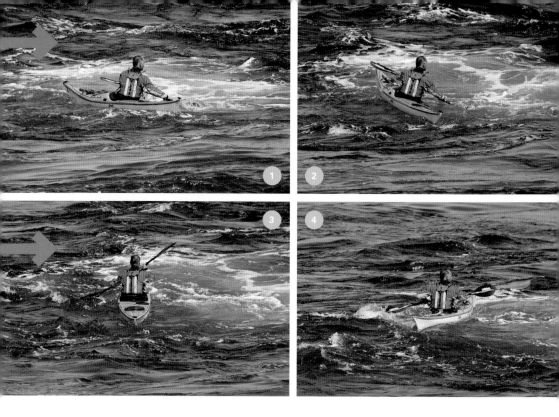

Tight turns in the flow

Often when out in the flow everything starts happening a little quicker than anticipated; the eddy arrives quicker or the rock or wave to be avoided is suddenly there. In these instances, a faster turn may be required. The kayak will be slowed down while executing a tight turn, which can often be useful. If there is limited time and a reduction in speed would be useful, use the following tight turn.

➡ *direction of flow*   ① + ②   Using the braced handbrake turn in the flow.

- Initiate a braced handbrake turn using a low brace.

- Start the brace as far back as is comfortable to give maximum turning.

- Move the bracing blade forwards to turn the kayak.

- Edge the kayak as much as feels comfortable; the more the better.

- Rotate your upper body towards the direction of the turn to help with the power transfer.

- Move the knees towards the braced paddle; this will maximise power transfer.

- Time the turn to make best use of any waves.

- Maintain the braced turn until the kayak comes to a stop and finishes turning.

3 + 4 Using sweep strokes to continue the turn if required.

- As the braced turn stops, initiate a sweep stroke on the opposite side if further turning is required.

- Reach as far forwards as is comfortable.

- Edge towards the sweep stroke as much as is comfortable.

- Look in the direction of the turn and push with the foot nearest the sweeping blade.

- Finish the sweep stroke when the paddle is level with the hips to help maintain stability.

- Repeat with further sweep strokes if more turning is still required.

- Use a skimming recovery stroke between linked sweeps to help with stability.

ENVIRONMENTAL CONSIDERATIONS

When ferry gliding, use the environment to assist in maintaining a straight paddling route across the flow (and therefore the correct upstream angle of the kayak). Before setting off into the flow, visually pick a point close to the shore being aimed for; then pick another feature that is behind this first point and lines up exactly with it. While ferry gliding keep looking towards these two points and ensure that they are kept lined up all the time. This will ensure that the kayak is not being moved downstream or downwind, and the ferry glide will therefore maintain angle perfectly. This technique is known as 'maintaining a transit'.

Ferry gliding across the main flow towards an eddy.
➡ *direction of flow*
➡ *ground track*

Forward ferry glide

When needing to move across a flow of water (or moving across a strong wind), it is important that the paddler does not lose any ground. To do this efficiently, the kayak must be lined up at a precise angle pointing up into the moving water or wind. By paddling at a constant pace, it will be possible to travel across the flow without being moved downstream or downwind. Being able to ferry glide efficiently is clearly an important skill to acquire; the last thing any paddler wants is to be ferry gliding out to a remote island and missing it!

- Before focusing on the ferry glide paddling technique, it is important to understand the bigger picture of how the ferry glide works.

- Identify the 'eddy' in the picture: this is the slacker water which the paddler is looking at.

- Identify the main flow in the picture: from left to right.

- Identify the 'eddy line' in the picture (i.e. the change from eddy to flow): the paddler is just approaching this.

- Use the above picture to help understand how the kayak is not pointing where the paddler wants to go, but in a direction to ensure the kayak maintains position across the flow.

- With the angle of the kayak set appropriately, the combination of forward paddling and the flow against the kayak moves it across the flow in a straight line.

COACH'S TOP TIP

Breaking in, breaking out and ferry gliding

Select your launch pad; this is where you set your angle, edge and speed depending on what you see in front of you. Remember eddy lines can be confusing and changeable; it is often very reactive paddling. Don't be timid; power and a positive attitude will often be the key. Look where you want to go and lead with both your head and shoulders.

When breaking out, think ahead about what part of the eddy you want to be in. Start lining up early as you can be caught out by the increase in speed as you get closer; use coastal features to judge your speed and then concentrate on your target. Eddy lines can be confused and aggressive, so speed and angle are important to drive through into the eddy.

To ferry glide set the angle, edge and speed at your launch pad. You still need to punch through the eddy line to get into the flow. Remember the speed of the flow will vary, so keep your eye on coastal features to judge speed and position. Keep the forward strokes going as you cross the eddy line before you apply a rudder. Don't forget the edge and keep the leading hand high on the rudder to start rather than leaning back; this creates a powerful lever for the rudder. Look where you are going.

Olly Sanders

A climber and a paddler, Olly has been expeditioning for over 20 years be it in the mountains or on the sea and was nominated in 2004 for the Piolet d'Or for a first ascent in Alaska. Qualified as a Level 5 Sea Coach and a MIC, he now runs his own coaching company after working full time at Plas-y-Brenin for 10 years. He has also produced three instructional DVDs on sea kayaking and climbing; another on expeditioning is due out at the end of 2011. For more information, visit *www.rockandseadventures.co.uk* and *www.rockandseaproductions.co.uk*.

➡ *direction of flow*
➡ *ground track*

1 Leaving the eddy while ensuring the speed, edge, position and angle are all correct.

● Use the slack water in the eddy to set up the angle and get speed on the kayak.

● Decide on the best position to leave the eddy; this is usually at the top of the eddy (i.e. at the most upstream part of the eddy) where the eddy line is cleanest.

● Good forward speed is required before crossing the eddy line; try to match the kayak speed to the speed of the oncoming flow (similar to when joining a motorway in a car).

● To get the kayak up to speed over a relatively short distant, use good high-angle forward paddling for power.

● Ensure that the angle is set perfectly before the bow of the kayak enters the flow.

2 + **3** Entering the flow and maintaining the ferry glide angle.

- As the kayak approaches the eddy line, set it on a medium downstream edge (i.e. edge the kayak away from the flow about to be entered by raising the upstream knee and looking downstream).

- Ensure this edge is constantly maintained while continuing to forward paddle.

- As the bow of the kayak starts to cross the eddy line, focus on maintaining speed, edge and angle of the kayak.

- In faster flows, the angle may change (as in the photo sequence) as the kayak initially crosses the eddy line; anticipate this to ensure the appropriate angle is possible once in the flow.

- To help with the above, try to time the final stroke in the eddy to be on the downstream side of the kayak in relation to the flow.

- This final stroke can be finished with a slight rudder to help maintain the direction across the eddy line.

- Ensure good power transfer is used with the final stroke, as it will then set the kayak up for the ferry glide.

4 Maintaining the ferry glide angle across the flow, looking where you are going.

- The angle the kayak is set at above could be described as 1 o'clock; perfect for this fast flow of water.

- It will take some experimenting to discover the appropriate ferry glide angles: the faster the flow, the smaller the angle from upstream (11 o'clock or 1 o'clock) and the slower the flow, the larger the angle from upstream (10 o'clock or 2 o'clock).

- Maintain constant forward paddling in the ferry glide; if correction strokes are required, this is an indication that the ferry glide angle is not correct.

- The speed of the water will change while crossing the flow; be prepared to change the ferry glide angle to accommodate this. Try to make these adjustments before you hit a change in water speed, or as soon as you notice a difference.

- Ensure a slight downstream edge is maintained; the faster the flow, the greater the edge is required.

- Keep looking in the direction of travel as opposed to looking at the bow of the kayak; this will help maintain the edge.

- By looking where you are going, it is possible to keep checking a transit to ensure that the angle and speed of paddling is efficient to cross the flow.

- If correction strokes are required, use strokes that turn the stern e.g. stern draw since the bow will be locked in the flow.

- Forward paddling is all that is needed when the angle is set correctly. If the kayak moves upstream of the transit ease off on the power, if it moves downstream then power needs to be increased.

TOP TIPS

When making reference to angles when approaching and crossing eddy lines, try using a clockface to help understand what angle is required; for example, 12 o'clock is always exactly upstream. To travel to the left or right, the kayak should then point towards 11 o'clock or 1 o'clock, respectively.

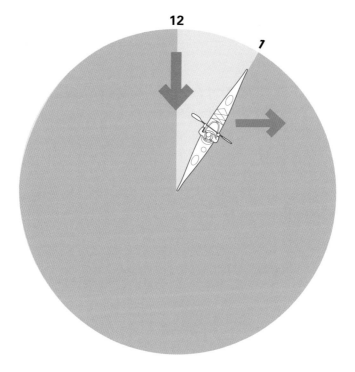

TOP TIPS

When carrying out any manoeuvre that involves crossing an eddy line, there are four key points to consider:

Speed

Edge

Position

Angle

Before heading off across an eddy line, think SEPA!

Reverse ferry glide

Reverse ferry gliding across any great distance would clearly not be very sensible. The reverse ferry glide is more often used as a method of maintaining direction or slowing down when already paddling with the flow. It gives the paddler the option to manoeuvre the kayak left or right by reverse ferry gliding to avoid obstacles, or set up for what is coming next.

 Reverse ferry gliding in the flow.

- Start the reverse ferry glide when in the flow by setting the correct angle and reverse paddling.

- The Speed, Edge, Position and Angle are the same as for the forward ferry glide.

- Set the angle either to hold position, change direction or move across the flow.

- Hold your position by changing the angle of the stern so that it either points upstream or is set at the opposite to the previous angle, e.g. move from 1 o'clock to 11 o'clock.

- Good reverse paddling technique should be easy to maintain if the angle is set correctly.

- Keep looking in the direction of travel, as opposed to the bow of the kayak, to help maintain edge and make use of transits.

- As it is not possible to 'see' everything that is happening, develop the ability to 'feel' how the water and flow is affecting the kayak.

- Due to the stern being locked in the flow, it is easiest to use turning strokes towards the bow of the kayak e.g. forward sweep strokes.

- While ferry gliding use transits to check on position; look over the downstream shoulder to help maintain the edge.

TOP TIPS

Ferry gliding and other manoeuvres in the moving water require the paddler to be very aware of the 'feel' of the Boat, Body and Blade in relation to the water. To develop this 'feel', try to maintain a ferry glide angle with your eyes closed while focusing on individual aspects of the three Bs. Also try this exercise while crossing the eddy line.

To achieve maximum efficiency, try ferry gliding a section of flowing water while using as few strokes as possible. Repeat while trying to reduce the number of strokes, then perhaps try this with eyes closed!

Breaking into the flow

Sooner or later it will be time to leave the eddy and join the main flow of water. For the experienced, this is when the fun starts and the tidal rollercoaster ride can begin. For the inexperienced, this can be a time for fingers crossed and hope for the best! It is clearly an essential skill to be able to leave an eddy, cross an eddy line and join the main tidal flow. What is more, this needs to be done efficiently and confidently. Depending on the size of the eddy, the speed of the water, how tight a turn is needed and the confidence of the paddler, there are a variety of options for breaking into the flow. In the following, we look at three main methods that will help the paddler break into the flow in any given situation.

Braced break-in

This break-in will become the default setting for most sea paddlers when needing to get into the flow. It offers stability along with the flexibility to be able to turn the kayak as tightly as is needed. For the beginner, it will provide confidence and efficiency; for the expert it will provide something that is guaranteed to work when the going gets really rough.

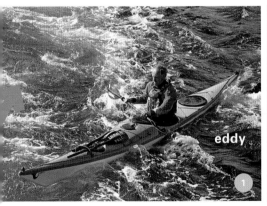

1. Getting the Speed, Edge, Position and Angle correct for breaking in to the flow.

● The Speed, Edge, Position and Angle for the braced break-in is as important as it was for the ferry glide, and is the key to success.

● As with the ferry glide, ensure the slacker water in the eddy is used to get SEPA correct for the braced break-in.

- To break in, the speed needs to be at least as fast as the oncoming water.

- The best position is usually at the top of the eddy, where the eddy line will be best defined and easiest to see.

- If the flow is too fast at the top of the eddy for the paddler's ability, then lower down will be slower and may be easier (but the ferry glide break-in described next may be better).

- A good break-in angle to start with is either 10 o'clock or 2 o'clock (depending on direction of travel). This is worth experimenting with; any angle nearer 12 o'clock will give a wider turn and any angle nearer 9 or 3 o'clock will give a tighter turn.

- Tighter turns are usually less stable.

- Good high-angle paddling speed needs to be used to start powering towards the eddy line.

2 Using the sweep stroke to start the turn in the braced break-in.

- Generate good speed with an angle of 10 or 2 o'clock while ensuring that the eddy line has been identified (in the photo the kayak is set to 2 o'clock).

- The turning part of the braced break-in needs to be started in the eddy just before the eddy line is crossed.

- As the bow of the sea kayak approaches the eddy line, initiate a turn with a forward sweep stroke until the paddle is level with the hips.

- This sweep stroke should be executed quickly to get the turn started just before the eddy line.

- To maximise the power in this quick stroke, the power transfer through the foot nearest the sweeping paddle needs to be very positive.

- Ensure the speed of the kayak is maintained; it should be similar to or faster than the oncoming water.

3 Using a good brace and edge to break in to the flow.

- As soon as the sweep stroke is finished ensure the kayak is now edged away from the flow about to be entered.

- The faster the flow, the bigger an edge is required and it must be set before crossing the eddy line.

- The kayak should still have plenty of forwards speed.

- As the kayak crosses the eddy line, the initial sweep stroke turn will now be assisted by the flowing water to complete the turn.

- To help with stability while crossing the eddy line, hold the paddle blade in a low brace position on the downstream side; this low brace is best positioned at about hip level.

- Ensure the front edge of the blade is slightly raised so it can skim the surface and provide support.

- From the sweep stroke initiation and throughout the turn, the body and head should be turned towards the direction in which the kayak is travelling.

4 Finishing the braced break-in, looking where you are going all the time.

- Ensure the edge is maintained throughout the turn, gradually released only when the kayak is pointing downstream and the turn is completed.

- This turn needs to be completed out in the main flow and not on the eddy line; if completed on the eddy line it will feel very unstable.

- If not completed in the main flow, then more speed is required on the approach or less power on the sweep.

- If a tighter turn is required, either change the approach angle or apply increased pressure on the bracing blade (even moving it towards the knees).

- Try not to stall the kayak in the turn, as this will lead to a loss of stability.

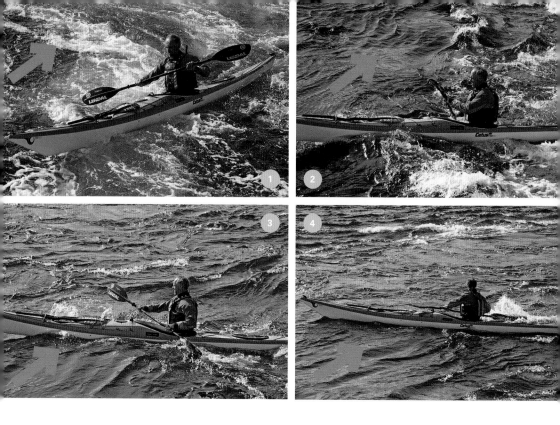

Ferry glide break-in

I have included this break-in as I have found it the most stable, efficient and easiest of them all on really big water, or for the beginner struggling to cross an eddy line with stability. Trying to turn close to the eddy line can be challenging as often the eddy lines can be very wide with a lot of confused water. To try to turn anywhere near this is arguably not the most sensible course of action. In essence, all this break-in does is ferry glide across and well beyond the eddy line, thus avoiding turning in this unstable area. Stable forward paddling can therefore be used in any confused water. When out in the flowing water, which is less confused, the ferry glide angle can be lost and used as a break-in to point downstream and continue the journey. The main limitation of this method is that it needs lots of space and does not produce a tight turn.

1 + 2   Using the ferry glide to get across the eddy line and into the flow.

•   The ferry glide to cross the eddy line is exactly as described previously.

- Remember to ensure the last stroke leaving the eddy is a powerful one on the downstream side.

- Continue this ferry glide until beyond the eddy line, where less confused water is reached.

3. Allowing the bow of the kayak to move downstream when in the flow, using a sweep stroke to help.

- When out in the main flow allow the ferry glide angle to be lost, so the kayak starts to face downstream.

- To help with this, a forward sweep stroke ending when the blade is level with the hips could be used on the upstream side of the kayak.

- In this instance there is no need to apply any edge towards the sweep stroke.

- If there are any waves, try to time the sweep stroke on the top of a wave.

- The sweep will not be needed in many cases; simply missing a forward stroke on the downstream side may be enough to start the turn.

- Turn the head and body towards the downstream direction to help with the turn, as well as to see what is coming up next.

4. Using a braced turn to finish and get the kayak pointing downstream.

- As soon as the kayak has started to turn downstream, apply a braced turn as described in the braced break-in.

- Slightly more edge will be needed than has already been used during the ferry glide.

- Apply more pressure on the braced turn if a quicker turn is needed, even moving the blade forwards towards the knees.

- Do not release the edge or flatten the kayak until pointing downstream and resuming forward paddling.

Bow rudder break-in

This is a more challenging stroke sequence to perform and does not provide as much stability as the techniques described previously. It is therefore fair to say that any sea paddler can go their whole life paddling in tidal races and never need this stroke, so becoming totally confident with the braced break-in is always going to be the recommendation. This said, if the paddler has the skill and confidence to do a bow rudder break-in, there could be some advantages in certain environments. These include: increased control of how tight the break-in turn is; being able to easily change how tight or how wide the turn is while on the move; being able to maintain momentum through the turn; and being able to convert the bow rudder into a forward power stroke when required.

PHYSICAL CONSIDERATION

Given the length of a sea kayak, the strains that can be imposed on the shoulder joint by an incorrectly applied bow rudder can be enormous. The key point to remember is that the bow rudder should only be applied once the boat is already turning. It is used to assist and increase the rate of turn, never to initiate it.

---

1 Crossing the eddy line, using a sweep stroke to initiate the break-in.

- The Speed, Edge, Position and Angle for the bow rudder break-in are exactly the same as for the braced break-in.

- The initiating sweep to start the bow rudder break-in is exactly the same as for the braced break-in.

2 + **3** Using the bow rudder to turn the kayak downstream in the flow.

- As with the previous break-ins, there must be good speed to carry the kayak across the eddy line and into the flow.

- As soon as the sweep is finished, ensure there is a good downstream edge to cross the eddy line.

- When crossing the eddy into the flow, reach forwards to plant the bow rudder into the main flow.

- Ensure the blade is fully submerged and the kayak is edged towards it.

- Turn the head and body towards the direction of travel.

- Initially have the bow rudder blade set at an angle that slices through the water rather than turning the kayak; this keeps speed on the kayak as it moves away from the eddy line.

- Slowly open up the angle of the blade so that it catches more water and turns the kayak tighter.

- By playing with the angle of the blade, the speed of the kayak and the shape of the turn can be controlled.

- Keeping constant pressure on the blade and a good edge will help with stability.

- Converting the bow rudder into a forward power stroke to keep the kayak moving.

- Maintain a constant edge and pressure on the blade until the kayak is pointing downstream.

- At this stage, the edge can gradually be reduced until the boat is flat.

- When the kayak is flat, the bow rudder can be converted into a forward power stroke.

- Use this power stroke to maintain stability and instantly start the kayak moving forwards.

TOP TIPS

For many paddlers, the challenge of breaking in is getting the correct amount of edge at the start and maintaining the right amount of edge all the way to the end of the break-in turn. To help with this consider the following. Imagine the kayak is a jumbo jet banking around a corner. It slowly comes onto an edge, is on its greatest edge at the top of the corner and slowly flattens off as it finishes the turn. Now paddle like a plane across the eddy line, flattening off when pointing downstream.

Alternatively, recall the 0–3 numbering system for describing amount of edge (see Chapter 6 of Sea Kayak Handling). Paddle a turn while changing from 0 (on the flat) to 3 (at the apex of the turn) in the sequence: 0–1–2–3–3–2–1–0. Now do the same while paddling across the eddy line (3 as the eddy line is crossed and 0 when pointing downstream).

Try both techniques with eyes closed to develop the feel for it.

Eddy line turn

The eddy line turn is a method of turning the sea kayak very tightly by using the main flow to turn the bow of the boat and the eddy to turn the stern of the boat. As the turn therefore takes place on the eddy line, stability is always going to be a consideration; this turn would therefore only be performed where the eddy line is very clean and flow is not too fast. The main reason for performing an eddy line turn would be because there is limited space to turn the kayak or it needs to be turned very quickly.

1. The bow in the flow and the stern in the eddy for a tight eddy line turn.

- Approach the eddy line slowly.

- As a tight turn is desired, the angle should be wide as the bow enters the flow (between 2 and 3 o'clock).

- Position the kayak so that only the front half of the kayak is in the flow; the centre of the kayak should be on top of the eddy line.

- A forward sweep stroke can be used as the bow enters the flow to help the turn.

2. The bow turned downstream with the flow.

- The kayak should be on a slight edge away from the oncoming flow.

- The back half of the kayak needs to stay in the eddy; it is therefore anchored as the flow quickly turns the bow downstream.

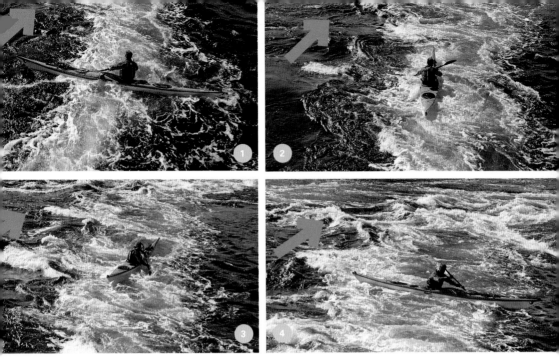

- Ensure the head and body are turned towards the downstream direction throughout.

- If support is needed, a brace can be used on the downstream side.

- As soon as the kayak is pointing in the direction that is required, forward paddle away from the eddy line into the flow.

- The eddy line turn can be continued to turn the kayak in a complete circle if required. This may be necessary in order to reposition in the eddy, or it can be used as a great eddy and edge awareness training exercise.

- **3 + 4** Continuing the eddy line turn so that the kayak turns back into the eddy.

- Use a reverse sweep to slow the kayak and turn the bow into the eddy.

- With the bow in the eddy the kayak will start to turn around.

- Ensure that the body is positioned over the eddy line.

- Assist the turn with a forward sweep.

- Look towards the turn.

- Use a small amount of edge as appropriate for stability.

- Try to develop the 'feel' for this turn.

TOP TIPS

An awareness of the eddy line and kayak is essential for all moving water skills. On eddy lines where the paddler feels very comfortable, there exists a great opportunity to set some challenges to increase awareness.

Eddy line spins: having completed the eddy line turn described, have a go at turning it into a spin by putting the bow back into the eddy while keeping the stern in the main flow. It should be possible to spin the kayak 360° until dizzy!

Reverse break-ins and break-outs: have a go at performing the break-ins and break-outs described backwards. This is a great challenge to increase awareness of SEPA.

For the ultimate challenge, try the above exercises with eyes closed!

Breaking out of the flow

When out enjoying the waves and rollercoaster ride of the moving water, at some stage a rest may be needed in an eddy. This may be to catch breath, access some great surf waves or to have a look at what is happening down tide. Whatever is the reason, it is important to be able to get into the eddy efficiently with a good degree of certainty. As with breaking into the flow, there are a few methods of breaking out as well as different circumstances in which it is best to use them.

Braced break-out

As with the braced break-in, this method will generally be the default setting for sea kayakers to efficiently get into an eddy. It provides stability as well as the flexibility to finish the turn as tight as is needed, so the paddler should end up sat just where they want to be.

1. Getting the Speed, Edge, Position and Angle correct for the break-out.

- As with ferry glides and break-ins, Speed, Edge, Position and Angle are key to breaking out of the flow into the eddy.

- Speed is easier to achieve when breaking out as the flow is assisting; aim to cross the eddy line faster than the speed of the flow.

eddy

- The best position to aim for is where the eddy line is cleanest, which will generally be at the top of the eddy. This should allow the break-out to finish in the slack water right behind the obstacle creating the eddy.

- The water may occasionally be surging in this area; if it is, aim for an easier position for the break-out. For breaking out, getting this position right is key to success.

- An angle nearer 5 or 7 o'clock will give a wider turn and an angle nearer 3 or 9 o'clock will give a tighter turn.

- In most instances, 4 or 8 o'clock is a good angle to set the kayak at ready for the break-out; in the photo the kayak is set to 8 o'clock.

- Using a sweep stroke just before crossing the eddy line to start the turn.

- With good speed on the boat, aim for the eddy line.

- As the bow of the boat approaches the eddy line, perform a forward sweep stroke to initiate the turn.

- A slight edge towards the sweep stroke may help; ensure this can be done in the flow.

- This sweep stroke should be a quick stroke just to get the turn started before the eddy line.

- To maximise the power in this quick stroke, the power transfer through the foot nearest the sweeping paddle needs to be very positive.

- Ensure the speed of the kayak is maintained, slightly faster than the flow.

eddy

3 + **4**   Using the low brace to turn the kayak as it crosses the eddy line.

● As soon as the sweep stroke is finished, the kayak should cross the eddy line.

● At this stage, change edge so the kayak is now edged up into the eddy, which will be upstream to the flow just paddled out of.

● The faster the flow, the greater the edge is required; this must be set up just as the eddy line is crossed.

● As the kayak crosses the eddy line the initial sweep stroke turn will now be assisted by the eddy to complete the turn.

● To help with stability while crossing the eddy line, hold the paddle blade in a low brace position on the up-eddy side. This low brace is best positioned at about hip level.

- Ensure the front edge of the blade is slightly raised so it can skim the surface and provide support.

- From the sweep stroke initiation and throughout the turn, the body and head should be turned towards the direction of travel up into the eddy.

5. Finishing the braced break-out in the eddy.

- Ensure the edge is maintained throughout the turn and gradually released only when the kayak is pointing up into the eddy and the turn is completed.

- This turn needs to be completed well within the eddy; if completed on the eddy line it will feel very unstable.

- If completed before you reach the eddy, then more speed is required on the approach or power on the brace should be reduced (too much of a brace has a slowing effect on the kayak).

- If a tighter turn is required, either change the approach angle or apply increased pressure on the bracing blade (think about moving the knees towards the blade).

- Try not to stall the kayak in the turn, as this will lead to it becoming less stable.

- It is best to time the Speed, Edge, Position and Angle so that the kayak comes to a stop pointing upstream in slack water at the top of the eddy, well away from any confused water.

Paddle in break-out

This is a similar concept to the ferry glide break-in. It keeps good speed on the kayak while crossing the eddy line, and the turn is complete when the kayak is on slack water well within the eddy. This break-out only works when entering a large eddy, but there are lots of these on the sea. If there is enough space in the eddy, this break-out gives plenty of stability as no turning takes place on the confused eddy line. Eddy lines are often big and confused, so adopting this break-out works well as you get to choose to turn when the water is at its calmest.

1. Approaching the eddy for the paddle-in break-out.

- Ensure the speed of approach is faster than the speed of the flow.

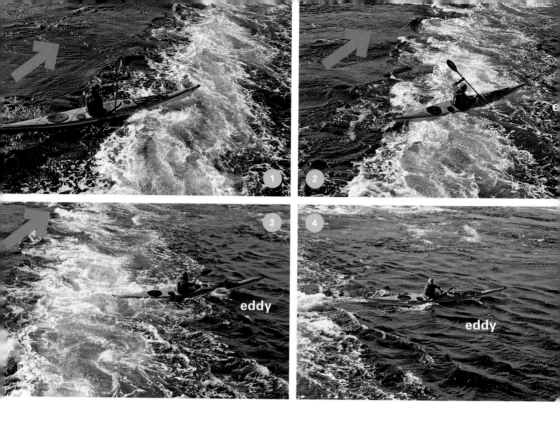

- No edge is required while approaching the eddy line; this helps to maintain speed, which is important.

- Position is key for this break-out; aim for an area with as clean an eddy line as possible which has plenty of room in the eddy beyond to paddle into.

- The angle is best set between 4 and 5 o'clock or 7 and 8 o'clock (in the photo the angle is set at 8 o'clock).

- Powering across the eddy line and using an upstream forward stroke to maintain speed and direction into the eddy.

- As the bow of the boat crosses the eddy line, it is important to keep forward paddling to maintain the speed.

- The faster the flow, the more confused the eddy and the faster the kayak should be paddled.

- As soon as the kayak starts to cross the eddy line, put on an edge towards the up-eddy direction. A small to medium edge will be required; again, the faster the flow the greater the edge.

- Use a powerful forward stroke on the upstream side as the kayak enters the eddy.

- The upstream forward stroke helps prevent the kayak turning and drives it into the calm water beyond the eddy line.

- The Speed, Edge, Position and Angle should be maintained until well inside the eddy and in calmer water.

3. Forward paddling into the calm water of the eddy before turning the kayak to point upstream.

- When the calmer water is reached within the eddy, the forward paddling can ease and stop.

- At this stage it is still best and most stable to get the kayak pointing up-eddy, which also sets the paddler up for exiting the eddy when required.

- To start this turn use a forward sweep stroke. A slight edge towards the sweep will help this turn.

- Ensure the head and body are facing up-eddy, along with good power transfer on the sweep stroke.

4. Using the braced turn to finish the turn in the calm of the eddy.

- To complete the break-out use a low braced turn.

- Edge well towards the bracing blade to help the turn.

- Have the front edge of the blade angled slightly up so that it does not catch.

- Apply as much pressure on the blade as is required to bring the kayak to a stop facing up-eddy.

- If more turning is required, move the blade from the hip position towards the knees and apply power transfer through the knees by lifting them towards the blade.

- When the kayak comes to a stop the edge can be flattened.

Bow rudder break-out

As when using the bow rudder for breaking in, this stroke offers less stability and is more technical to perform than the break-outs already described. The advantages are also similar, in that the bow rudder break-out gives greater control on how tight the turn is and can be easily converted to a power stroke if needed. This can be of particular use when breaking out as, once in the eddy, power is often needed to move the kayak up-eddy towards the calmest water.

COACH'S TOP TIP

Always look to where you want to go – not just in the general direction, but to the exact spot you want to be at. As you begin to set up for the break-out, your focus needs to switch from sea mode (taking in the big picture, the wind, waves, weather, group, your feelings) to whitewater mode with complete focus on that eddy. Not unlike a fighter pilot you lock on to the target, visually to the eddy and physically to your kayak, allowing you and your kayak to 'fly' as one into the eddy. Power forwards all the time as you cross the eddy line and into the top of the eddy.

Similarly, before you set off when breaking in and ferry gliding, lock on visually to the future water then 'launch' yourself and kayak into the flow. Wherever you look, your boat will follow; the better connected you are, the easier the boat can move with you. Push

through your feet engaging maximum power, angle and edge, transferring power to the kayak so it can blast your way through the turbulence of the eddy line.

Trys Burke

Trys is a BCU Level 5 Sea Coach who also enjoys river running, canoeing and flying. She is a freelance coach for Canoe Wales, Surf-Lines and Bangor University, along with sea symposiums in the USA, Norway, Finland and the UK. She is a committed expedition paddler. Trys is married to Simon and has two boys, Finlay and Caden.

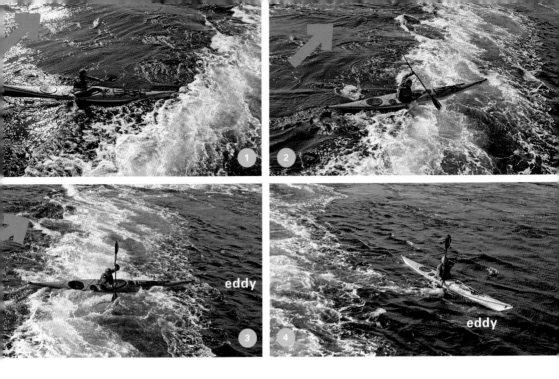

Getting lined up to cross the eddy line and using a sweep in the flow to start the turn.

- The Speed, Edge, Position and Angle for the bow rudder break-out are exactly the same as for the braced break-out.

- The initiation sweep to start the bow rudder break-out is exactly the same as for the braced break-out.

2 + 3   Planting the bow rudder beyond the eddy line to turn the kayak.

- As with the previous break-outs, there must be good speed to carry the kayak across the eddy line and into the eddy.

- As soon as the sweep is finished and the bow crosses the eddy line, change to an up-eddy edge.

- When across the eddy line, use a bow rudder to continue the turn.

- Plant the bow rudder beyond the aerated eddy line. Ensure that the blade is fully submerged and the kayak is edged towards it.

- Turn the head and body towards the direction of travel.

- Initially have the bow rudder blade at an angle that slices through the water rather than turns the kayak; this keeps speed on the kayak as it moves into the eddy.

- Slowly open up the angle of the blade so that it catches more water and turns the kayak tighter. By playing with the angle of the blade, the speed of the kayak and the angle of the turn can be controlled.

- Keeping constant pressure on the blade and a good edge will help with stability.

4. Converting the bow rudder into a forward power stroke when the turn is finished in the eddy.

- Maintain a constant edge and pressure on the blade until the kayak is pointing up into the eddy.

- At this stage the edge can be gradually lessened until the boat is flat.

- When the kayak is flat, the bow rudder can be converted into a forward power stroke if required. Use this power stroke to maintain stability and start the kayak instantly moving forwards.

ENVIRONMENTAL CONSIDERATIONS

When paddling in moving water, wind will have a big effect. If the wind is against the moving water it will become a lot rougher; if going with the moving water it will flatten the waves. The moving water skills will not change; however, choosing a technique which offers more stability may be wise in conditions of wind against tide.

If it is windy, once in the moving water turn the kayak using the same tactics as described in the 'High wind paddling' chapter. Since the kayak will be moving at a similar speed to the water, the wind will have a greater effect. If it is not windy, use similar techniques to turn as for non-moving water. If there are waves, however, try to turn on the top of these to make it easier.

TOP TIPS

It is worth reflecting on the chapter considering the TTPP model; use this to set goals for the main areas that need to be improved upon. Here are some key TTPP areas from the chapter. Use these as a start and add more depending on the skill being focused on.

TACTICAL

Speed.
Edge.
Position.
Angle.

TECHNICAL

Vertical shaft of bow rudder.
Holding an even edge while forward paddling.
Looking in direction of travel during the turn.

PHYSICAL

Power in forward paddling.
Power in sweep stroke.
Flexibility in turns.
Endurance.

PSYCHOLOGICAL

Confidence in moving water.
Attentional focus on eddy line.
Self-talk prior to break-ins.
Managing arousal levels.

SURFING

Surfing a sea kayak is an essential skill for all sea kayakers to have. When journeying with a following sea, some basic surf skills will allow a lot of energy to be saved. On this same journey, when landing on a beach with surf all around those same surf skills could lead to a dry and safe end to the day as opposed to a wet and injured end.

Some surf knowledge is essential for everyone, however a bit of time spent developing these surf skills can also lead to a world of fun. Out on the tidal races or with a big following sea, the sea kayak has the speed to come alive on waves where most other kayaks would be left behind. It is playing in the tidal races where a sport in itself is developing, and it is here where the sea kayak is best used for surfing.

It is of course also possible to enjoy surfing the sea kayak on the beach, reef or point breaks around the coastlines. That said, these waves are often too fast and steep for the sea kayak; hence the evolution of the surf kayak. If you have tried surfing in these places and enjoyed it, take what you have learnt, buy a surf kayak and go have some more fun. In this chapter, we look at the skills required to get the most from a range of surf environments.

Beach break surf launching

Identify the peaks and the best launching areas in the photo above bearing in mind the following points:

- Tactical choice of where to launch or land is the key to success.

- Identify where the waves start, so the safe zone out beyond the waves can be used.

- Look for areas that have no rocks or similar hazards.

- Identify where the waves are regularly breaking (peaks), seen by the consistent inverted 'V's of white.

- Look for areas of calmer water between these peaks.

- Identify the bigger waves as they come in and how regular they are; these are known as 'sets' and usually arrive in groups of about three.

- Look for areas of water flowing away from the beach (rips); there will be fewer waves here and sometimes slightly confused surface water.

- These rips are often at the edges of the beach (there is one in the picture along the cliffs) where streams flow into the waves, yet can also be anywhere along bigger beaches.

- Rips can make paddling out very easy and can sometimes be easier to paddle in against than trying to surf in.

- Look for where the water flows parallel to the beach close in (longshore drift/rip).

- These rips can make getting in and out of the kayak very awkward.

- All rips are potentially dangerous if swimming in them.

1 + 2   Launching from a beach out into the surf.

- Having observed the beach, launch where there are fewest waves.

- Identify if the tide is coming in or out, as this helps with the tactics.

- Ensure all loose equipment on the deck is well secured so it is not lost and there is no chance of it becoming entangled.

- With an incoming tide, get into the kayak just above the tide line (so you have of time to get sorted as you wait for the tide to come in).

- With an outgoing tide, wait for a set to go through then move the kayak as far out as possible so it is just in the water; get in quickly and wait for the next set.

- As the waves come in they will catch the bow of the kayak first, turning the kayak sideways into an unstable position.

- To prevent this, use the paddle and hand to keep the kayak pointing straight.

- Once the wave starts to pick up the kayak, use the paddle and hand to push out.

3 Watching breaking waves to get the timing right for paddling out.

- Timing is key to paddling out through waves.

- Use the calm between the waves to paddle out as fast as possible; high-angle forward paddling is best for this.

- Identify where the waves are breaking and where they are at their steepest; time the paddle out to avoid these.

4 Careful timing to avoid the breaking white wave.

- To avoid the breaking waves it is sometimes best to slow or even stop to allow a wave to break ahead of you.

5 Reaching forward while paddling through a breaking wave.

- When paddling through a wave, lean well forward.

- Accelerate as much as possible into the wave.

- As you are going into the wave, focus on planting the next forward paddle stroke beyond the breaking wave.

- Once the forward paddle stroke is planted beyond the wave, apply constant power transfer on it to pull though the wave.

- Look away from the wave as it breaks to keep the face clear of water; this helps see what is following the first wave as soon as it clears.

- If the wave starts to take the kayak backwards, hang on the planted forward stroke to try and anchor the kayak and let the wave pass.

- If this does not work, be prepared to adopt a safe braced position (covered in the next section).

1 + **2**   Capsizing and waiting for the wave to pass.

- If the wave about to break looks too big to paddle through, consider rolling.

- With a big wave there is a risk of back looping or being capsized out of control; both these can lead to injury and should be avoided if possible. Rolling in front of the wave can protect from this.

- Stay tucked up in a strong safe set up to roll position.

- The extra drag of your body under the water can anchor the kayak and let the wave pass by.

3 + **4**   Rolling up in the calmer water when the wave has passed.

- Roll up when the wave has passed by.

- When finishing the roll, ensure a forward paddling position is adopted as soon as possible; start paddling immediately as there may be another wave coming.

- If the above has happened, focus a little more on the timing to avoid the breaking waves!

The kayaker staying within the 'safety box' in a variety of strokes.

THE SAFETY BOX

The kayaker's 'safety box' is a key part of paddling that everyone needs to be aware of. When out kayaking and performing any skills, the paddler needs to ensure that no part of the upper body is overextended; this is particularly important with the additional forces involved with long sea kayaks. The safety box is an imaginary box within which the upper body needs to stay. If at any stage in a stroke the hands extend above the shoulders or to the side where the elbow is more than two-thirds extended, then they will be out of the 'safety box'. Awareness of this box prevents overextending (particularly arms and shoulder joints) which could perhaps lead to an injury.

Beach break surf landing

Having the skill to land safely on a surf beach at the end of a day's paddle with a loaded sea kayak is essential. The power of the surf combined with the long levers of kayak and paddle mean that there are a lot of possibilities for injury if care is not taken. There is also nothing worse than getting it wrong at the end of the day and arriving at the campsite a soggy mess. Here are some considerations to help perfect that dry-hair landing.

1. Waiting in the 'safe' zone and watching the waves.

- Identifying the 'safe' zone beyond the break is the essential starting place; use transits on the land to maintain position in the area.

- From the safe zone it is important to decide the best route to land through the surf.

- When deciding the above, consider rocks, rips, where the waves are breaking most and where on the beach it is easiest to land.

- While in the safe zone get a feel of how regularly the waves are coming in and the timing of the sets (a series of usually 3–4 bigger waves).

- Before leaving the safe zone, agree upon who is going when, that everyone has plenty of space, a method of communication (hand signals) and what should happen if someone capsizes and swims.

- Looking behind you to help time the landing between the waves.

- The art to safely landing with dry hair is to get to the beach without catching a wave!

- Time your forward paddling so that you can paddle to shore on the backs of the waves.

- To help with the timing of paddling on the backs of the waves, keep a constant look at what is behind you.

- If there is someone on the beach then they can help with this (using agreed signals).

- Once a wave has passed under the kayak, use powerful high-angle forward paddle strokes to get in as far as possible.

- Try to time your paddle in towards the beach so that all paddling occurs between sets of waves.

3 + **4** Paddling backwards through a wave to ensure it passes under the kayak.

- To paddle on the backs of the waves, the waves must be allowed to pass under the kayak on the way in. To help with this, slow down the forward paddling as they approach.

- If these waves have already broken, then ensure forward paddling is stopped.

- Start paddling backwards towards the approaching broken wave.

- Ensure that the stern of the kayak is always kept at exactly right angles to the approaching wave.

- As the broken wave picks up the stern of the kayak, use a couple of extra powerful backward strokes.

- At this stage, move the upper body so that it is upright or slightly backwards; this helps to ensure that the wave does not pick up the kayak.

- Maintain the backward strokes until the wave has passed.

- At this stage check that there are no more immediate waves approaching; if there are, continue reverse paddling.

5 Start paddling on the back of the wave as soon as it has passed under the kayak.

- As soon as the wave has passed under the kayak and there are no more immediately following, start the forward paddling on the back of the wave as already described.

- If the wave catches you while backward paddling then a capsize may follow; if this is the case, then go for a roll as already described.

- If a roll fails and a swim follows, ensure that the kayak is kept between the beach and you. This means that, if another wave comes, the kayak will not be pushed on top of you but will be pushed safely away from you.

- If the wave has caught you, then you may also now be surfing! See the following section of this chapter for how to maintain control of the kayak.

- If surfing in the broken white wave, see the section later in this chapter on 'Surfing the soup'.

6 + **7**   Step out of the kayak as quickly as possible when landing.

●   When landing the sea kayak, ensure that it is kept at right angles to the beach.

●   If it is sandy then the kayak can be run ashore and the following steps carried out (if it is not sandy, then the following steps will need to be carried out while afloat).

●   Release the spray deck and get one leg out of the kayak. Time this so that there are no waves approaching.

●   As it becomes shallow enough or the kayak has landed on the sand, step out of the kayak. Use the paddle and the kayak to help this.

8   Take hold of the kayak and move it away from the surf as quickly as possible.

●   Quickly move to the bow and pull the kayak above the surf line.

●   The ability to step out of a kayak like this is key for awkward landings.

●   Some kayak cockpits are not large enough for this to be possible, if this is the case then the less stable method of sliding the backside up onto the rear of the cockpit will need to be used.

EQUIPMENT CONSIDERATIONS

Certain sea kayaks will perform better in the surf environment than others; in fact, there are now some more play-orientated sea kayaks on the market. A shorter sea kayak with a more rounded hull and less of a keel line will generally perform better in the surf and tidal races.

Consider the length of the paddle, as this can also make things easier. A shorter paddle will make it easier for the fast and more dynamic strokes required; a larger blade can also help to maximise the power of the shorter strokes being used.

Surfing the soup

There is no doubt that when landing or out surfing you will end up in the 'soup' at some stage: this is the white broken wave. It is important that you gain the skills to be in control in the soup. Going out to practise these is a great way to start developing confidence and awareness in the surf environment. I would strongly recommend becoming confident with the following skills before trying to surf the green waves.

Side surfing

No matter how skilful you are, at some stage the wave will take control of the situation. When it does you will often end up in a side-surfing position, also known as the 'bongo slide'. This is when you are side-on to the broken white wave and being moved towards the beach. This can often lead to a capsize for the unaware; however, with practice, it is possible to stabilise a side surf and then either get off the wave or turn to start surfing the broken wave.

1 + 2   Maintain a good safe low brace on the wave.

● Ensure a good low brace position is used (think about the safety box).

● Try to maintain the bracing blade on top of the broken wave.

● Maintain a good edge towards the broken wave, gaining support from the low brace.

- To help with the stability of the brace position, keep the body as far forward as possible.

- Maintain this position until the waves start to get smaller and die away.

- Keep looking towards where the wave is taking you to see any hazards.

- While bracing, it is possible to add small forward or reverse strokes to the bracing blade to move forwards or backwards along the wave to avoid hazards.

3. A high brace on the wave (everything within the 'safety box').

- If the wave is large then a high brace may occasionally need to be used; the above safety considerations are the same for this.

- As soon as is possible, convert the high brace into a low brace.

TOP TIP

In really big waves it may not be possible to do a high brace on top of the wave without hyper-extending your shoulders. In these situations, stab the paddle blade into the face of the wave (this is usually done in a high brace position). Ensure that at all times the brace is well within the 'safety box' and hands are no higher than shoulders. This done, hold your breath and hope for the best!

 Converting the low brace into a draw stroke to get off a wave when side surfing.

- To get off the wave, maintain the edge but change the low brace to a draw stroke.

- The draw stroke needs to be placed in the water behind the breaking wave.

- Use this draw stroke to anchor the kayak, thus letting the wave pass under the kayak.

- Placing the draw stroke slightly forwards can have a turning effect on the kayak, helping to getting off the wave.

- Ensure the blade is placed deep in the water.

- Use good power transfer through the up-edge knee by pulling it towards the drawing blade and engaging core muscles; this will maximise the power and help draw the boat towards the anchored paddle.

- Turning the bow of the kayak towards the wave can make it easier to start using forward paddle strokes to paddle off the wave.

Surfing

It is also possible to use the soup to surf in towards the beach; this may happen when landing as a wave from behind catches you up. If side surfing, it is also possible when drawing off the wave to turn the kayak so you can then surf the white waves into shore.

1   Positioning the kayak on top of the soup.

- Once the white wave is not too steep (this usually happens fairly quickly after the wave has broken), try to position the kayak towards the top of the soup.

- To do this a few reverse strokes can work, slowing the kayak down to allow the wave to catch up.

- Once towards the top of the broken wave, it will be easier to turn the kayak to ensure it points in the direction you want to go.

- The bow and stern of the kayak will be free of the wave, which is why it is easier to turn.

2 + **3**   Surfing the soup towards the beach.

- Leaning slightly forwards and a few forward strokes can help at this stage.

- The kayak will accelerate down the wave.

- Remember to use forward and backward trim to help speed up or slow down the kayak and maintain control.

- The sea kayak will then quickly outrun the broken wave and you can forward paddle to safely land on the beach on the back of the wave in front.

- To help keep the kayak pointing towards the beach, use a stern rudder.

TOP TIPS

Spending time practising in the soup is a great way to gain confidence and skills for surfing. Try side surfing with your eyes closed to get a better feel for the balance and body position. Challenge yourself by trying to side surf with as little pressure on the bracing blade as possible – can you side surf without a bracing blade? Once comfortable side surfing, try to move the sea kayak forwards and backwards along the wave (by moving the brace further forward or further back) while being side surfed; again, can you do this with eyes closed?

Beach break surfing

Having the skills to surf a wave as it comes into the beach is clearly going to be useful when landing in surf (and a lot of fun as well). Whether it is surf on a beach, over a sand bar, a rocky reef or off a point, the skills used are all the same. Waves formed like this are usually steeper and faster than out on the open sea or a tide race, and on these waves a long sea kayak is always going to be at a disadvantage compared to a shorter more manoeuvrable surf kayak. That said, there is still plenty of fun to be had and techniques to consider.

To help getting started in surfing, it will be useful to understand some simple surf language and what makes up a wave.

A classic surf break.

- The white water is the broken wave that becomes the soup.

- The area where the white turns into green is known as the shoulder.

- The high point of white from which the shoulder forms is known as the peak.

- The shoulder will usually run left or right, thus giving a left- or right-hand break.

- Quite often the peak will not form high enough and the shoulder will very quickly just form a broken wave; this is known as a wave 'closing out'.

- The steepest part of the shoulder right next to the white is the optimum place to surf; this is known as the pocket.

Catching a wave

Catching a wave is possibly the most important skill of surfing; it will often dictate the outcome of the ride in on the wave. It takes time and experience to know which wave to choose and where best to be positioned to catch it. The key aspect however is that you choose the wave and maintain complete control, as opposed to the wave picking you up and taking you for a ride. A few considerations to help with this are listed in the following.

1 + 2 + 3   Choosing a good wave and catching it with the kayak angled away from the beach.

- Choose a wave that is not too steep and has an obvious peak forming that will give a clean shoulder.

- Having chosen the wave, decide whether it is best to surf left or right on it (this will usually be away from the peak that is forming a shoulder).

- As the wave starts to pick up the back of the kayak, ensure that the kayak is not pointing straight towards the beach. Pointing towards the beach means that (at best) you just outrun the wave or (at worst) the nose of the kayak will be driven down (potentially leading to damage to the boat or paddler).

- With the kayak angled slightly to the left or right, ensure you lean forwards as the wave picks up the stern.

- Use a few powerful short and fast high-angled forward paddling strokes to accelerate onto the wave.

- If the angle of the kayak or chosen direction is not correct, ensure that you change this as the wave is just picking up the kayak.

- Changing direction just as the kayak is being picked up is the easiest time to turn, as the bow and stern are out of the water at this stage.

4. Surfing the green wave with the kayak angled along the wave using a skimming low brace for support as needed.

- As soon as the kayak is picked up by the wave, stop forward paddling and move the body into an upright/slightly forward standard posture.

- The kayak should be angled along the wave, ideally away from the shoulder.

- To get maximum speed, the pocket is the perfect place to now be; a skimming low brace can provide support at this stage.

- Maintain an edge towards the wave face.

- Once the kayak is up and running, it is time for the diagonal run.

Diagonal run

Real surfing takes place on the green face of the wave, as opposed to the white broken wave known as the 'soup'. Surf kayaks are designed to do this effectively using their flat hulls, edges and fins. A sea kayak does not have these however, and the increased length and keel of a sea kayak is going to limit the amount of turning which can be done on a green wave. The diagonal run is a surfing manoeuvre that the sea kayaker can enjoy, however.

1   The diagonal run, looking along the wave with a skimming low brace for support as needed.

●   Once on a green wave, a diagonal run will give the best surf for a sea kayak.

●   The aim is to stay as high up on the green wave face as possible, while surfing along the wave away from the white shoulder.

●   Some edge will help the diagonal run, so after the take-off apply some edge towards the wave face.

●   If too much edge is used, the sea kayak will just turn up and off the wave.

●   Using the correct amount of edge and trim, the diagonal run can sometimes be maintained with a skimming brace.

●   Due to the sea kayak having a keel and not as much edge as a surf kayak, it can be difficult to stop it pointing up-wave and surfing off the back.

●   If this is the case, a down-wave stern rudder can help.

2 + 3   Using a down-wave stern rudder to help maintain the diagonal run.

●   To compliment the slight edge, a stern rudder can be used to help the sea kayak travel along the wave.

●   This stern rudder is usually placed on the down-wave side of the kayak to be of most use in keeping the kayak from turning off the wave.

●   If you need to turn higher up the wave while diagonal running, release the stern rudder and apply more edge if needed.

●   If needing to turn down-wave while diagonal running, apply pressure on the back of the blade of the stern rudder and lessen the edge.

- Moving up and down the green wave face is known as 'climbing and dropping', this is the same terminology as for surf kayaks and boards.

- Use your body to trim the kayak forwards to increase speed and backwards to slow down.

- If more of a turn down the wave face is required, consider a top turn.

Top turn

Due to the length of keel line on a sea kayak, it is not really possible to turn on the wave face; if any turning is going to be done in a sea kayak it therefore has to happen at the top of the wave. Some of the keel will be out of the water at the top of the wave, and turning will therefore be easier. To perform a classic top turn and go from diagonal running in one direction to running in the opposite direction (as shown in the photos below) is going to be very hard in most sea kayaks. It is more likely that the top turn is used to just turn the sea kayak to get it pointing back down the wave while travelling in the same direction on a diagonal run.

1 + 2   Converting the stern rudder into a powerful stern pry to start the top turn, using the correct timing.

- Position the kayak on the top of the wave.

- By releasing the stern rudder and edging a bit more towards the wave while in a diagonal run, the kayak will move towards the top of the wave.

- Timing is important here, as there is very little time before the wave has passed and the kayak has fallen off the back of the wave.

- As the centre of the kayak approaches the top of the wave, the bow will start to rise out of the water.

- At this point move the body as far forward as possible.

- At the same time, convert the stern rudder into a very powerful stern pry by moving it directly away from the stern of the kayak.

- To help with the power, engage the core muscles and think about dynamically moving the hips and backside away from the paddle.

3 + 4 Transferring the edge with forward body movement to start surfing in the new direction.

- Use a dynamic edge transfer towards the stern pry; the more edge used the easier the turn will be.

- To avoid falling off the back of the wave, keep the body weight as far forward as is possible.

- Follow the stern pry with powerful forward strokes if further speed is required to stay on the wave.

- The kayak should now be diagonal running in the new direction.

Getting off the wave

Knowing how and when to call it a day on a wave and get off is a sign of experience. All too often kayakers will either stay on the wave too long and end up getting trashed in the breaking wave, or catch a wave which is too steep and breaks instantly. Knowing when to back off when catching a wave or get off a wave before it breaks is an essential skill to learn if you are to enjoy green wave surfing.

1 + 2   Backing off a breaking wave which is constantly steep and breaking.

- When catching a wave, look left and right along it to see if it is good to catch or is constantly steep along the entire length.

- If is it constantly steep there will be no shoulder to surf, it will just break to white.

- It is time to back off the wave and let it pass under the kayak; use powerful reverse paddle strokes.

- Move the body backwards to help prevent the kayak being picked up.

- Keep putting in these powerful strokes until the wave has passed.

- At this stage immediately check behind; there may be a better wave coming to catch.

3   Exiting the wave at the end of a diagonal run.

- It is important to be able to exit off a wave safely when surfing the green.

- If caught in the white water then the kayak will often end up side surfing (described earlier in the chapter).

- The best way to get off a wave is while there is still forward speed.

- With this forward speed, totally remove any stern rudder and apply as much edge towards the wave as is possible.

- Move the body as far forward as possible as the kayak turns up-wave, all the time trying to maintain the speed.

- Using a skimming brace towards the wave can add support and help the turn.

- As soon as the bow starts to go through or over the wave, reach forward with a forwards paddle stroke to catch the water behind the breaking wave.

- This reach forwards may involve punching the top paddle hand through the wave.

- At this stage the body and head will be well forward; keeping the head down stops getting too much of a face full of water.

- Once the forward paddle stroke catches the water behind the wave, apply gradual force on it to pull the sea kayak off the wave.

- Follow this with further forward paddle strokes to get fully off the wave.

- Remember to look up and check out what is behind the exited wave – it may be an even bigger one!

Other users: sharing the surf

Surf is a popular environment and inevitably there can be a lot of people wanting to make the most of it. Of all those out enjoying the surf, the sea kayaker is perhaps the least manoeuvrable of them all and we therefore have the biggest obligation to other surf users. Commonsense will hopefully allow everyone to have a good time out in the surf, but here are a few things to consider.

Above: Sharing the surf with other users.

- When practising surfing, choose the emptiest beach as is possible. (In sea kayaks it should be easier for us to find such locations as paddling to a remote beach is easy.)

- If there are other users give them lots of space.

- Only ever surf a wave if there is no one else on it.

- If two people are going for a wave, the person nearest the shoulder has right of way. If unsure, get off.

- If it is not clear where the shoulder is going to form, whoever is up and running on the wave first has right of way. If unsure, get off.

- Sea kayaks can catch waves a lot further out than other surfers, but don't catch all the waves; let plenty go through for the boarders.

- Before taking off, check that you have a clear run in to shore and not a surfboard slalom.

- If caught sideways in a wave, keep a constant look to where you are being swept; there may be someone in the water.

- If you think you may collide with someone get out of the way as quickly as possible.

- If you can't get out of the way then capsize: this will stop the boat and thus protect yourself and hopefully the other person.

- Do not paddle out through the area where people are surfing in.

- Chat, smile and be friendly. This can go a long way to gaining respect and understanding.

TOP TIPS

The surf environment can either fill the paddler's mind with terror or excitement; with a few tips, that terror should soon grow to excitement. Often it is the perceived unpredictable nature of the surf or lack of control, especially in a sea kayak, which causes the terror. The length of the average sea kayak means it is not designed for technical manoeuvres; however, it is possible to move beyond the bongo slide. The key is to be pro-active and to plan your paddling out and surfing in.

Adopt an upright posture. Keep key strokes within the safety box and favour the low brace, as this keeps the body in a position more likely to prevent injury.

For steering, use a combination of edge and deep rudder strokes behind the hip. Once the kayak is within the wave it is difficult to control; however, some element of control is available by adjusting body trim. Slowing the kayak to get the stern to release at the top of the wave improves manoeuvrability.

Tide race and following sea surfing

The waves formed by tidal races or when there is a following sea are the waves that a sea kayak will come to life on. They are generally longer, less steep and with a constant fast speed; the sea kayak is therefore the perfect tool for the job. For this reason many paddlers now go looking for these environments to perfect their skills and enjoy the excitement of surfing a sea kayak.

As with all exciting environments, care needs to be taken and the correct skills need to be mastered. The skills for surfing a tidal race or a following sea are interchangeable; the main considerations are listed in the following.

ENVIRONMENTAL CONSIDERATIONS

Most tide races are relatively safe in good weather. As the tidal stream rushes past a point it starts as calm water, speeds up as it goes over the shallower water off the point, becomes rough as the overfalls form where the fast flow hits the slower deeper water and then becomes calm again. If someone comes out their boat, you can just follow them until they reach the calm water and perform a deep water rescue there.

Most tide races follow the general direction of the coast so if you have to wait for the calm water to perform a rescue, the land is not much further off than where you were playing. Be aware however that there are some tide races that flush straight out to sea. Another consideration is that if there is a strong offshore wind blowing and anything goes wrong, you will be drifting steadily out to sea.

In really rough weather, all bets are off. When the already rough sea hits the tidal race it turns into a mass of unpredictable, steep and nasty waves. We are talking raw survival in these conditions.

Tide race tactics

When heading out to a tidal race to surf some waves there are a lot of things to consider. Tidal planning and safety are essential for a successful day, in addition to the skills described in the 'Moving water' chapter. Consider the following if you want to make the most of the surfing.

1 Tidal race and waves with the perfect eddy for access.

● Not all tidal races form good surfing waves; seek out some local knowledge to help.

● There will be certain times of the tide, swell or weather conditions that provide the best waves; try to work this out or again seek local knowledge.

● Always get to a tidal race early while the waves are still building, allowing you some time to warm up to the environment.

● When it gets too big and scary – get off!

● Look for waves that have a nearby eddy, as in the picture.

● Use this eddy to access the waves and as a safe zone.

● Look out for others; 'one wave, one paddler' is the golden rule.

2 Watching the waves to see where the peak is forming.

● Spend time watching the waves to see how they form and work.

● Identify the peak, wave face and trough on the waves.

● The above are all essential to maximise your surfing and be able to manoeuvre on the wave.

3 Ferry gliding out to catch a wave, watching the waves all the time.

● It is generally easiest to start catching waves by ferry gliding out from an eddy to the waves at the upstream part of the tidal race or overfalls.

● Watch the waves around you and, in particular, the one you are trying to surf.

- Choose waves to surf that you are comfortable with; back off the bigger or steeper ones.

- In addition to this, develop a 'feel' for the waves and the environment.

Catching a wave

As when catching a wave on a beach break, this is the crucial part of surfing and will be the make-or-break part of the performance. You need to have the skill to choose the correct wave and then catch it in a way that allows you to have control of which way you want to go, how fast you go and how far you want to surf for.

1 + **2** Choosing a good wave and catching it using a few powerful strokes and forward trim.

- When catching and surfing a wave, the peak, wave face and trough are all used tactically to help control the kayak.

- On a tide race and on the sea the waves will come in sets (a group of waves slightly bigger than others); these can be used to help get the best surfing.

- Spend a bit of time getting a feel for when the bigger waves come through and where (or if) they are breaking.

- Having chosen the wave, decide whether you want to surf straight or go in a left or right direction.

- You will see the water fall away in front of the kayak; this is the time to start paddling.

- As the wave starts to pick up the back of the kayak, use a few powerful short and fast high-angled forward paddling strokes to accelerate onto the wave.

- Ensure that your body is well forwards.

3 Getting the kayak lined up to start surfing the wave.

- At this stage you will be on top of the wave; this is the time to put in a quick short sweep stroke if wanting to go left or right on the wave.

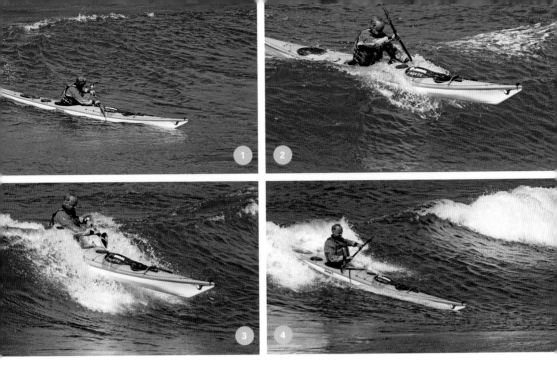

- Changing direction just as the kayak is being picked up is the easiest time to turn, as the stern is out of the water at this stage.

- As soon as the kayak is picked up by the wave, stop forward paddling and move the body into an upright/slightly forward standard posture.

- Surfing the wave using the body to trim the kayak and help control the speed.

- Try not to outrun the wave, but speed up or slow down to keep the kayak on the steeper wave face.

- Use the body to forward trim to speed up and backward trim to slow down.

- On a following sea, you often will not be able to get the kayak moving fast enough to catch this first wave.

- Use the speed generated trying to catch the first wave to catch the following wave in the same way as described above.

- Tactically, it can save energy to plan to use a wave just to generate speed before catching the next wave.

5 + 6   Catching a steeper wave with the kayak pointing too much down the wave face – oops!

- On steeper waves avoid catching the wave with the kayak straight down the wave face.

- This will bury the nose of the kayak, at best be unstable and, at worst, lead to capsize.

- This is the way to produce 'pop-outs' (when the kayak pops vertically out of the water due to the buoyancy of the bow)!

7   Surfing diagonally away from the peak on a steeper wave.

- To avoid the above happening, surf steeper waves on a diagonal.

- Try to surf away from the peak, as seen in the photo.

- To surf on a diagonal, remember the crucial quick short sweep stroke if wanting to go left or right on the wave when catching it. This is best done when the stern is free of the water.

COACH'S TOP TIP

The key to surfing any kayak is to mentally isolate your various body positions while on the wave. Isolate your fore and aft trim from the twisting of your hips and the rotation of your upper body when possibly applying a ruddering type stroke.

Your upper body weight is effectively your accelerator. Lean forwards to increase speed and descend down the wave face; lean back to slow down, stall the kayak and in effect rise back up the wave face. Once the kayak has speed, the twisting of your hips allows you to edge the kayak and efficiently steer in the direction you want to go. Your ruddering stroke gives power to this movement and helps keep you on track. Although these postures and positions work in isolation, the skill is to blend them together into one seamless movement which is continuously adapting to match the rhythm of the sea at that particular moment in time. This allows you to utilise as much energy from the wave as possible.

Howard Jeffs

Howard has been sea kayaking for nearly 40 years and in 1983 became the youngest BCU Level 5 Sea Coach of the time. Although very fortunate to have paddled all around the world, his love for the diverse west coast of Britain still remains strong. As well as an author, sea kayak designer and manufacturer and a mountain instructor, he is also an enthusiastic yachtsman. Visit him at *www.howardjeffs. com* or contact him at h.n.jeffs@btinternet.com.

8. Taking care with trim and direction when catching a big wave.

- On big steep waves it is not about leaning forwards and paddling hard to catch it; allowing it to pick you up at the top of the wave before the surf ride starts is crucial.

- Keep control of the kayak with good upright posture.

- Keeping looking and feeling the wave to help decide which way and how to surf on it.

- Make the decision and then choose to start the surf ride, as opposed to letting the wave take you.

Maintaining direction on a wave

Once up and running on a wave, the stern rudder becomes the key stroke to control the kayak. I would generally recommend having the skeg up while surfing and controlling the kayak using the stern rudder and kayak edge. This gives maximum flexibility to adapt the stern rudder quickly if required to make direction changes while on the wave. This may not be the case if you are journeying in one direction with a consistent following sea and not wanting to change direction; here the skeg may assist and save some energy. Being able to adapt the stern rudders while on a wave allows the paddler to keep constant control of the wave and the kayak. Using the wave face for speed and wave peak to turn is essential; adapting the stern rudder can help with the positioning to do this.

1. Stern rudder and rear trim to surf in a straight line, soon outrunning the wave.

- The high-angle stern rudder is used to keep the kayak running straight on the wave face.

- The high-angle stern rudder gives maximum power and control when surfing.

- The higher angle also allows the stroke to be adapted more easily if needed.

- Ensure the blade is fully submerged.

- Body rotation helps this; check that both hands are out over the water.

- Leaning back allows the stern rudder to be placed further back.

- Leaning back also trims the kayak to anchor the stern; if just wanting to go in a straight line this is fine. By going in a straight line the kayak will often outrun the wave.

- This can be a good tactic to use; however, if you want to be able to turn the kayak with the stern rudder to stay on the wave, leaning back is not ideal.

2. Stern rudder with upright body position to maintain better control of the kayak and also allow turning if required.

- A more upright body position with a stern rudder will provide more control of the kayak.

- Ensure good rotation is still used and the blade is fully submerged.

- This can still be used to keep the kayak travelling in a straight line.

- If turning is required the boat and body are in a good position; the stern is less 'locked' and the body can use the core muscles.

- The added control provided by the more upright stern rudder will allow you to keep the kayak on the wave face as opposed to just outrunning the wave.

Turning on the wave: top turns

The easiest place to turn on the wave is at the top of it when the stern is free of the water. When surfing a sea kayak, the majority of turning needs to be carried out when the boat is in this position. Aim to be in constant control of the kayak when surfing so that you have the option to turn the kayak with maximum efficiency. It is also important to be aware of when you will not be able to get the kayak in this position (usually on the bigger or steeper waves). When this is the case the take-off is even more critical, as the direction you choose to go will be the way you are then committed to.

1. Having the stern of the kayak free of the water allows for an easier turn.

- When catching the wave there will always be a period when the stern is free and a top turn can be used.

- When surfing the wave, slow the kayak down to get to the top of the wave and free the stern; leaning back a bit and dragging the stern rudder is the easiest way to do this.

- The optimum position to be in is where the paddler is sat up on the highest point of the wave.

With the stern of the kayak free a powerful stern pry will turn the kayak.

● When in the optimum position it may help to lean forward a little; this will release the stern further as well as help to stay on the wave.

● To initiate the stern pry turn, push the stern rudder away from the kayak powerfully ensuring that you use core muscles.

● Think about moving the knees in the direction of the turn to help with power transfer.

● As well as moving the knees, think of moving your bum away from the stern pry using the core muscles.

● There should be the feeling of a lot of torque in the body during this power transfer.

● Edging towards the blade can also help.

● Carry out the stern pry turning stroke quickly and dynamically so that it does not drag you off the back of the wave.

3 Surfing in the desired direction, using a skimming brace for support or further turning as required.

● When the turn is complete, continue surfing the wave.

● While starting to surf keep edging towards a lightly braced paddle to get a bit more turning; this also helps with balance when starting off surfing.

● Remember to lean forwards if acceleration is required to stay on the wave.

● If wanting to slow down and not outrun the wave, lean back a little (as in the photo).

Turning on the wave face

Once up and running on the wave, the kayak will be travelling at a good speed. To slow this speed down and turn on the top of the wave is one option, although it may often be difficult to do. To be able to turn on the wave face or towards the bottom of the wave is therefore another useful skill. This turn still needs to be on the wave as opposed to in the trough; once in the trough, the stern and bow of the kayak are often anchored in the water making it very hard to turn. There are a few ways to turn on the wave as described below.

1 + **2** Using a bracing stern rudder on the side you want to turn towards on the wave face.

● A braced stern rudder is the stroke that provides maximum stability as well as having a turning effect.

● Ensure the bracing stern rudder is on the same side as the direction you want to turn towards.

● It may be possible to convert the stern rudder being used to maintain direction into a bracing stern rudder.

● Keep the body as upright as possible to avoid 'locking' the stern and so the core muscles can be used.

● Hold the bracing blade as far out from the boat as is comfortable, but do not overextend the shoulders.

● Gradually increase the pressure on the bracing blade to turn the kayak.

● Look in the direction that you want to turn.

③ Using a good inside edge with the bracing stern rudder to maximise the turn on the wave.

● To help release the stern and bow of the kayak apply edge towards the blade (the inside edge of the turn).

● An inside edge turn is when the kayak is edged towards the blade and towards the inside of the turn (the kayak is turning left in the photo).

● Edging towards the bracing blade should feel stable.

● The more edge that can be applied, the easier the kayak will turn.

● To help with the power transfer and to engage the core muscles, think of lifting the up-edge knee towards the direction of the turn.

④ Using an outside edge to turn on longer less steep waves.

● On long waves that are less steep, an outside edge turn can be considered.

- An outside edge turn is when the kayak is edged away from the blade and towards the outside of the turn (the kayak is turning left in the photo).

- The kayak is in effect sat in the water the same as when paddling on the flat; the outside edge turn can therefore be very efficient.

- The outside edge turn will be a more gradual turn than the inside edge turn described already, so works best on long waves (often found with a following sea).

- Edge the kayak to the outside of the turn away from the stern rudder.

- Maintain good upright posture and knee connectivity in the kayak to help with this.

- Apply gentle pressure on the back of the stern rudder blade; pushing it away from the kayak slightly will help the turn.

- Push with the down-edge foot to maintain stability as well as help with power transfer.

- Look in the direction of the turn.

Bracing on a wave

When out enjoying the surf, sooner or later things may not quite go to plan. To avoid a potential capsize, the trusty support strokes may well need to be deployed. As already mentioned in the beach break surfing section, always go for a low brace whenever possible. When out surfing the bigger waves, the high brace may be the only answer however.

- 1 Bracing on the breaking wave, keeping everything within the 'safety box'.

- Ensure everything stays within the kayaker's safety box.

- Ensure that the arms, shoulders and body are not overextended in any way and that there is plenty of room for manoeuvre.

- Use the drive face of the paddle blade in the high brace.

- Keep the paddle placed on top of the broken wave.

- Maintain constant pressure on the paddle and support from it.

- Ensure the kayak is edged well towards the bracing blade.

- Maintain an upright body and head to help maintain balance and control of the kayak.

- By edging towards the blade, it stops the kayak tripping up on itself while being moved sideways by the broken wave.

- Puffing out your cheeks and closing your eyes has also been known to help!

- Maintaining the braced position until the wave dies away.

- The broken wave always dies away with time; maintain the braced position until this happens.

- Be aware of what you are being swept towards in case this represents a hazard (although the surfing venue should have been chosen with no exposed rocks).

- When the broken wave has disappeared, look around for the best place to paddle away to.

EQUIPMENT CONSIDERATIONS

When out in the surf on a beach or any environment where a bang on the head could be possible, I would recommend wearing a helmet. Even if there is deep water and no rocks around, remember that other kayakers could also be a hazard.

ROCK HOPPING

Rock hopping includes both manoeuvring as efficiently as possible on a flat calm day in between the tight rock gardens, caves, arches and sea stacks of a rocky coastline as well as playing among the rocks and swell while pushing the limits of what can be done without damaging boat or body; it is possibly the ultimate test of a sea kayaker's skill. It requires that perfect blend of strokes, edge control, timing and a complete understanding of the environment to succeed. When it all goes right, the paddler comes away with a feeling of mastery of both environment and craft.

The great thing about rock hopping is that the paddler can decide the challenge; no matter their ability, there is a lot of fun and learning to be had. Choose a calm day to start with and focus on just the kayak manoeuvring; add some gentle swell as confidence increases. The key to successful rock hopping is a tactical understanding based on using the environment and the best combination of strokes in the tight and dynamic locations.

Tactics

If going in close to rocks when there is a bit of swell and tidal movement it is essential to fully understand the environment, the effect the water will have on the kayak and how this can be used to help with manoeuvring or avoiding hazards. No matter how good the kayaker's strokes and paddling skills are, if the timing is wrong the environment will always win. Getting the tactics right is essential.

Spending time in the environment is key to understanding it, but the most important skill to learn is patience. Before heading into a rock-hopping manoeuvre, spend time watching what is happening with the sea and how it will affect what you are planning to do. Have the patience to sit and watch through at least one set of waves so a decision can be made on whether it is safe, when it is best to paddle and what to expect.

While you are observing the rock-hopping environment, look for ways in which the sea can help whatever manoeuvre is planned.

Timing of surges

Using the surge from the swell and good timing for a successful rock-hopping manoeuvre.

- The surges caused by the incoming swell can be used to get over shallows or rocks when rock hopping.

- These surges can be used to generate speed.

- Use forward/backward trim to speed up or slow down on the surge.

- These surges often come in 'sets' of two or three.

- Consider letting the first surge go through and using the second surge; this can help with timing and gives you a visual on what to expect after the first surge.

- If the second surge is missed, then there is still hopefully the third to catch.

- Depending on your ability or the gap to be paddled through, also look to be able to avoid surges.

- Time the paddle with when the water is at its calmest between surges, if it helps (there are some gaps that can only be paddled through in the relative calm between surges).

- Patience and watching will be the key to timing.

Using sideways surges

1 + 2 + 3 + 4   Using the sideways surge to gain speed and turn the kayak.

- Look for sideways surges that can help or hinder a manoeuvre.

- Use timing to either avoid these or use them.

- Develop the skill to know how these will affect the kayak.

Using eddies

 Breaking into an eddy behind a rock, formed by surging swell.

- Look for positions of safety when in close and rock hopping, either eddies or areas of calm water.

- Eddies form behind rocks when the water is surging; these provide good areas to stop and are relatively safe from surges.

- Use these areas to rest, watch and plan.

- Tactically plan to move from one area of safety to another.

- Use these calmer areas to get the kayak turned or lined up for the next part of the rock-hopping journey.

- Using the eddy itself can help with turning the kayak.

- Skills from the 'Moving water' chapter will help you to use eddies effectively.

Using the flow

Using the flow formed by swell surging in towards the gap to help the bow rudder turn.

- Look to see which way the water flows in and out with the surges.

- Use this flow of water to help with turns and manoeuvres.

→ direction of flow

- Focus on timing to help with this.
- Skills from the 'Moving water' chapter will help with this.

Close in to the rocks

1. A rock-hopping playground with safety and danger side by side.

- In the above photo, where would you go in close and where would you avoid?
- Spend time watching what happens when the water is aerated or non-aerated around rocks.
- Non-aerated water is usually good to go in close with.
- Aerated water needs to be treated with care; look to see where it is breaking to form the aeration.

- Learn how the waves that have not broken will pass under the kayak.

- Identify waves that are getting steep enough to break.

- Breaking waves will not pass under the kayak and can push you onto the rocks.

- Avoid being in close with breaking waves.

- If a breaking wave starts to come in, paddle straight out through it where possible.

- If caught side-on to a breaking wave, use a brace and draw blended stroke (see later in chapter).

- By becoming confident in the above decisions, you should be able to be relaxed when close in to rocks.

Techniques: blending strokes

When manoeuvring the kayak through the rocks and waves, there are no new strokes that are required in addition to what we have already looked at in Sea Kayak Handling. The difference is that, due to the dynamic environment and the tight spaces in among the rocks, strokes are often blended together for maximum effect. This is not too dissimilar to the way some of the strokes have already been blended in some of the previous chapters; when playing among the rocks the strokes often need to be performed with more skill and precision, however.

Stern rudders

When moving through narrow gaps where there is not enough room to forward paddle or put in turning strokes, the stern rudder is the main stroke for keeping control of the kayak. It can be used to maintain a straight line or steer the kayak if a small turn is required. To maintain an active paddle and constant control of the kayak, blending it with the forward paddle stroke can help.

1 + **2**   Converting a forward power stroke into the stern rudder.

- Use a high-angle forward paddle stroke to maximise acceleration and power.

- Keep the blade submerged at the end of the stroke and continue into the stern rudder position.

- Ensure good rotation so that both hands are outside the kayak and over the water.

- Use a high-angle stern rudder for maximum control.

- Use appropriate edging of the kayak and feathering of the blade to steer the kayak.

3 + 4 Slicing the stern rudder back into another power stroke to generate momentum in a tight space.

- When steering through a gap, the kayak may slow too much for the stern rudder to be effective.

- To help with this, convert the high-angle stern rudder back into a forward power stroke on the same side as the stern rudder.

- Ensure both hands stay outside the kayak and the paddle shaft is as vertical as possible.

- Keep the blade in the water and slice it forward into the catch phase of the forward paddling stroke.

- Put in a forward power stroke to gain speed.

- If enough speed is gained in one stroke, a stern rudder can be used again.

- If further speed is required and the gap is very narrow, slice the blade forward again for another forward power stroke on the same side.

An active blade in action.

TOP TIPS

When close-quarter manoeuvring in among rocks, aim to have a constantly 'active' paddle blade. Always have a blade in the water and keep control of how much pressure there is on the blade; this will ensure that you always have the ability to instantly be in control of the kayak. This active blade is essential to help maintain position and line up while waiting for the perfect rock-hopping moment. A vertical paddle gives the most flexibility; think of using the blade like a 'feeling' stick.

To help with this try closing your eyes and drawing a square in the water with the blade constantly submerged. Do this first without any pressure on the blade so that it is constantly slicing, and then try it with constant pressure on the blade. This will help to develop the blade awareness required for an active paddle and blended strokes.

Bow rudders

Bow rudders work well when needing to constantly make fine adjustments to a turn in tight spaces. This is due to the vertical paddle shaft allowing the kayak to be moved when there may not be space for wide sweep strokes. With the blade constantly active in the water, instant refinements can be made to maintain control of the kayak while turning as well as it being in a versatile position to be blended with many other strokes.

Bow rudder with forward paddle stroke

In the tight and dynamic environment of rock hopping, keeping speed on the kayak is often of high priority. The bow rudder allows for the kayak to be turned while maintaining forward momentum. By keeping the speed going after the turn, a forward power stroke can be linked.

Turning the kayak during the break-in with a bow rudder, then converting it into a forward power stroke to maintain momentum.

- Use the bow rudder to turn the kayak as much as is required.

- Remember to edge the kayak, look into the turn, apply power on the foot and maintain constant power on the blade for the turn.

- When the turn is complete release the edge on the kayak.

- Move the bow rudder blade in towards the side of the kayak.

- Convert the bow rudder into a high-angle forward power stroke, as if it was the catch phase.

- Start the forward paddle stroke power phase to move the kayak forwards.

Bow rudder with bow draw

The bow rudder will only have a turning effect on the kayak when there is forward momentum. If the kayak stops turning due to a lack of forward movement, then the bow rudder can be blended with a bow draw to keep turning the kayak.

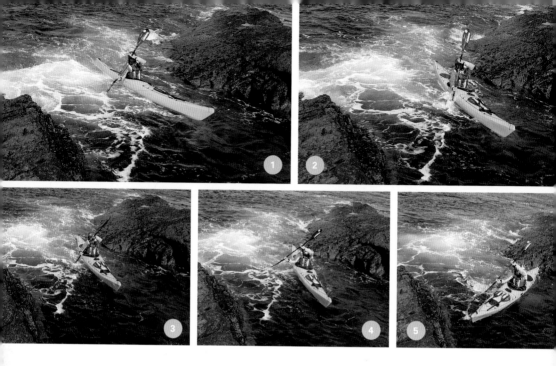

1 + 2   Finishing the bow rudder by blending it with a bow draw for increased turning.

- Use the bow rudder to turn the kayak (remembering the safety box and that you must have already initiated the turn with a bow sweep or another stroke).

- Remember to edge the kayak, look into the turn, apply power on the foot and maintain constant power on the blade for the turn.

- When the kayak stops turning due to lack of forward speed, maintain the edge on the kayak.

- With the blade in the bow rudder position, draw it towards the side of the kayak keeping it as far forward as is comfortable (usually about level with the knees).

- Ensure the blade is fully submerged.

- Use core muscles along with power transfer through the feet and knees to power the blade towards the kayak.

3 + 4 + 5   Slicing the bow draw back into the bow rudder position so another bow draw can be used.

- If further turning is required, slice the blade back out to the bow rudder position.

- Maintain the kayak on an edge; it may feel more comfortable to edge towards the blade at this point.

- Once the blade is back in the bow rudder position, perform another bow draw as described above.

- If more turning is required, repeat this process.

- If the turn is complete and forward momentum is needed, convert the bow draw into a forward paddle stroke as described in the previous section.

Bow rudder with sweep stroke finish

The bow rudder with bow draw works well in very tight places; however, there is a limit to how much turning can be done with the draw due to stability and strength. If there is enough space, a better way to get more turning when the bow rudder stops having an effect is to combine it with a sweep stroke.

 Once the bow rudder has finished turning the kayak, carry out a sweep stroke on the opposite side if further turning is needed.

- Use the bow rudder to turn the kayak (remembering the safety box and that you must have already initiated the turn with a bow sweep or another stroke).

- When the kayak stops turning due to a lack of forward speed, maintain the edge on the kayak.

- Move the paddle into a forward sweep initiation position on the opposite side of the bow rudder.

- When initiating the sweep, angle the blade slightly to get some support from the power face.

- Edge the kayak towards the sweep stroke as much as is comfortable.

- Remember to drive with the foot nearest the blade, use core muscles to help power transfer and sweep the blade in an arc at arm's length from the kayak.

4 + **5**   Repeat with additional sweep strokes if required, link these with a skimming recovery stroke for stability.

- If further turning is required, use additional sweep strokes.

- To help maintain edge and stability, consider using a skimming recovery stroke in between linked sweep strokes.

- Keep looking in the direction of the turn and applying pressure on the foot nearest the sweep stroke.

Bow rudder with stern draw finish

Although a bow rudder is used at the start of this blend of strokes, the outcome is to move the kayak sideways as opposed to turning the kayak. Generally a hanging draw or draw on the move is used to move a sea kayak sideways, a skill that is often used when rock hopping. If a sideways movement can be anticipated when looking ahead, try blending a bow rudder to move the bow and then a stern draw on the same side to move the stern of the kayak. This can have more of a sideways movement effect then the draw strokes, as well as being fairly quick to perform.

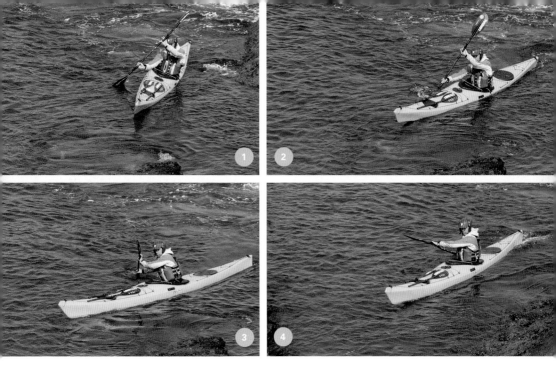

1 + **2** Using the bow rudder to move the bow of the kayak away from the obstacle and converting it into a forward power stroke.

- Use the bow rudder to turn the kayak (remembering the safety box and that you must have already initiated the turn with a bow sweep or another stroke).

- When the kayak stops turning due to a lack of forward speed, drop the edge on the kayak.

- Convert the bow rudder into a power stroke as previously described.

- Finish the power stroke at the hips.

3 + **4** Slicing the forward stroke towards the stern and then using a stern draw to move the stern of kayak away from the obstacle.

- When the forward paddle stroke is at the hips, slice it out and towards the stern into a stern draw starting position.

- Edge the kayak towards the stern draw as much as is comfortable.

- Draw the blade in towards the side of the kayak as far towards the stern as is comfortable.

- Apply as much power as is comfortable and as is required to straighten up the kayak.

- The kayak should be back in a straight running position, having been moved sideways by the bow and stern strokes.

- If the kayak is not running straight, perform a further stern draw.

TOP TIPS

Spend time practising all these blended strokes in calm conditions with plenty of space first. Once they are mastered like this, try doing them with eyes closed to get the feel for them before challenging yourself by doing them in rougher conditions. Once comfortable in rougher conditions, put them together in a rock-hopping environment.

Spend plenty of time patiently watching the rock-hopping environment before committing to kayaking within it. This will help you to understand how the waves and swell interact and the effect they may have on the kayak.

Braced turns

Although the bow rudder is a very adaptable stroke to use when rock hopping, it does not provide the most stable of turning strokes and often does not provide as tight a turn as an inside-edged-braced turn. When among the rocks, a tight turn that will not lead to a capsize is often the ideal; having a more stable turning stroke is therefore essential. For this, the braced handbrake turn works very well for those tight turns in rougher conditions, when losing speed on the kayak does not matter.

Braced turn with sweep finish

The braced turn works well on its own; in tight spaces it can however be blended with a sweep stroke to get more turning from the stroke. This is easy to do as at the end of the braced turn the kayak will have come to a natural stop.

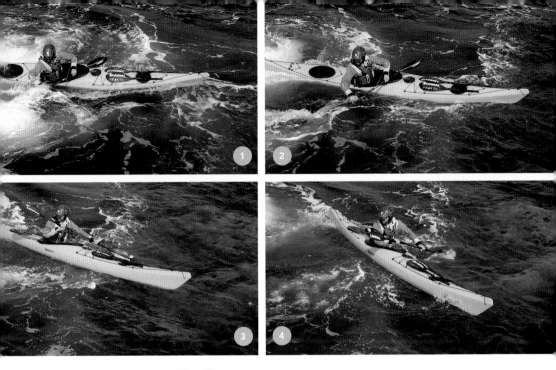

1 + 2 Using a braced handbrake turn to enter an eddy formed by the swell.

- Ensure the kayak is travelling at a reasonable speed.

- If the kayak needs to stay tracking in a straight line, initially consider using a stern rudder.

- When needing to turn, carry out a braced handbrake turn.

- If using a stern rudder, convert this into the bracing part of the turn.

- Maintain the braced turn until the kayak slows and stops turning.

- Remember to initiate with a sweep stroke and look in the direction of the turn if not using a stern rudder.

- Apply constant pressure on the blade and move it from just behind the hips to near the knees. Think about moving the up-edge knee towards the braced blade for increased power transfer.

- Keep the kayak on as much edge as is comfortable towards the braced blade.

- Maintain the brace until the kayak slows and the turn stops.

3 + 4 Changing the edge and finishing the braced turn with a sweep stroke.

COACH'S TOP TIP

The inside edge turn does not see much action on the open ocean, where boat speed and gradual changes of direction are often more useful. Among rocks and breaking waves, however, it is a vital component of effective and accurate boat handling. If we need to turn quickly and precisely, the inside edge turn (if performed well) is a great option.

Practise gliding between two rocks with a stern rudder locked cleanly in the water; make sure you've got good body rotation and a fully immersed blade. Now unwind your upper body, driving the active blade away from the side of the kayak in a wide arc towards a point level with your hips. This creates a turning effect that can be increased by edging progressively into the turn towards the active blade, to increase the kayak's manoeuvrability.

As the active blade reaches a point level with your hips, flatten the kayak and sit upright ready for the next move. If performed effectively, your kayak will have turned quickly through 90° and, at the end of the move, be stationary in the water.

The key to success is dynamic edging: keep your upper body in front of your hips and commit your bodyweight to the inside edge of the kayak. You can also angle the back of the active blade slightly downwards for increased support. Once you've got the move nailed on open water, it's time to take your new skills into a more dynamic environment. Let's go rock hopping!

Nick Cunliffe

Nick is a BCU Level 5 Sea Coach from North Wales who has been involved in sea kayaking, coaching, guiding and adventure paddling throughout the UK and overseas for over 20 years. A great paddling day for Nick will always be in the tide races of his Anglesey home waters. Nick offers sea kayak training courses through Kayak Essentials, and also produces canoe sport training DVDs including his latest production *Sea Kayak Essentials*; see *www.kayakessentials.co.uk*.

- When the kayak starts to come to a stop, change the brace into a sweep initiation on the opposite side.

- Change edges at the same time so that the kayak is now edged towards the new sweep stroke.

- Carry out a powerful forward sweep, remembering to drive with the foot and look towards the turning direction.

- If further turning is required, follow the forward sweep with a reverse sweep on the opposite side (as for a 360° static turn).

Braced turn with bow draw finish

Having turned the kayak with a braced turn, there may not be enough room to follow it up with a sweep stroke if further turning is required. In this case, a bow draw can be used. With practice, this may well become a more flowing and effective stroke than using a sweep. By being able to stay on the same edge while keeping constant pressure on the blade, more stability can be obtained.

- **1** + **2**   Using a braced handbrake turn to enter an eddy formed by the swell.

- Carry out a braced turn as already described.

- When the kayak begins to slow down, reduce the amount of edge.

3 + 4   Converting the braced turn into a bow draw if more turning is needed.

●   Keeping constant pressure on the back of the bracing blade, move it forward into a bow draw starting position.

●   When in position, move the paddle shaft into the vertical bow draw start position.

●   Apply pressure on the front of the blade when it is moved into the bow draw, helping to provide stability.

●   Draw the blade in towards the kayak to continue the turn.

●   Add further bow draws if more turning is required.

Hanging draws

When paddling in and out of rocks in tight spaces, moving the kayak sideways is often needed. Assuming there is some forward speed, then the hanging draw works perfectly for this. As there is constant pressure on the blade (as for the bow rudder), it gives constant control of the kayak and of the speed and size of the sideways movement. If speed is lost during the hanging draw, it is of course easy to convert it into a standard draw stroke. In addition to this, it is easy to blend the hanging draw into another couple of useful strokes.

Hanging draw with bow rudder/draw or forward power stroke

While in the hanging draw position, it is easy to slice the blade forwards to give options of blending the draw with a bow rudder/draw if a turn is required or into a forward paddling stroke if continued speed is needed.

 Using the hanging draw to move sideways away from a rock.

● Use a hanging draw to move sideways.

● Remember to initiate the draw by placing it on the same side as the last forward stroke taken, as well as slicing it forward from the end of that extended stroke.

● Ensure the body is well rotated, the paddle is as vertical as possible and the kayak is edged towards the draw stroke.

 +  Slicing the hanging draw forwards into a bow rudder and power stroke, moving the kayak away from the rock.

● Once enough sideways movement has been achieved, keep the body well rotated and slice the blade forwards as far as is possible.

● Moving the body forwards with the paddle can help with this.

● If a turn is required, slice the blade forwards into a bow rudder/ draw position.

● If forward paddling is required, slice the blade forwards and into the forward paddle stroke catch position before starting to forward paddle.

Hanging draw with stern draw or rudder

If after having moved the kayak sideways a slight turn is required away from the drawing paddle side, then blending the hanging draw with a stern draw works well. If a straight course is instead required and the kayak still has forward speed, then blending the hanging draw into a stern rudder is a good option.

1 + 2 Finishing the hanging draw and slicing the blade backwards to initiate a stern draw.

- Use the hanging draw to move the kayak sideways.

- Slice the blade backwards towards the stern of the kayak as far as is comfortable; the blade will now be at the initiation position for the stern draw.

- To help with this, rotate the body as much as is possible and move the lower hand further back than the upper hand.

- The upper hand will be lower than when performing the hanging draw.

- Keep the blade a relaxed arm's length away from the kayak as with the hanging draw.

3 + 4 Using the stern draw to move the stern away from the rock and change direction, the blade getting set for another stroke.

- Remember to apply pressure on the blade, edge towards the stern draw and push the top hand away from the kayak to help with this.

- Add additional stern draws if more turning is required.

- If a stern rudder is required, slice the blade in a similar way but into the stern rudder position.

*A low brace support
on a surge.*

Low brace supports

When close into the rocks and surrounded by confused water, sooner or later a low brace stroke will be required. This should be the bread-and-butter support stroke (as discussed in Sea Kayak Handling), preventing the need for high braces or even a roll. Apart from staying dry, the other advantage of the low brace is that it can be blended with other strokes easily: blending it with the forward paddle stroke will get you out of the environment you are bracing in, or blending it with the draw stroke will help pull you off a sideways wave you may be bracing on.

Low brace with forward paddle stroke

Having been forced to use a low brace, moving away from whatever feature caused you to use it will most probably be a high priority. Quickly changing the brace into a forward paddling stroke will be ideal for this. Another consideration is that forward paddle strokes add stability to the kayak.

   Bracing and then moving the blade ready for the forward paddle stroke initiation.

- Carry out a low brace stroke to regain stability of the kayak.

- As the brace is finished, rotate the wrist to slice the blade out of the water.

- As the blade is slicing out of the water, slice it in a forward direction as opposed to straight out as with a standard low brace.

- As the blade slices forward, rotate the body slightly towards the blade to help with this.

- Once the blade is out of the water, it should be almost lined up for the forward paddling stroke.

3 + 4 Using a powerful forward stroke to move away from the obstacle that required a brace.

● Move the blade further forward as required with increased rotation, to get it into the forward paddle stroke catch position.

● Start the forward paddle stroke.

Low brace with draw stroke

Another situation in which a low brace may be required is when you are caught by a sideways wave or swell. The brace will work well to support against the wave; to get off the wave which may be moving the kayak sideways, however, a draw stroke may be required.

1 + 2 + 3 Bracing onto the swell and then blending it with the draw stroke to move off the swell and away from the rocks.

● Perform a low brace on the top of the wave or swell for support.

● Maintain an edge towards the breaking wave and the low brace for increased stability.

- When able to, maintain a balanced edge towards the wave and convert the brace into a draw stroke.

- Try to place the draw stroke in non-aerated water beyond the wave.

- Hold the draw stroke initiation position; support should still be gained from the pressure on the blade as the kayak is being moved sideways by the wave.

- Ensure good rotation is used and look towards the draw stroke.

- Maintain connectivity to help with the edge control.

- The kayak may be drawn off the wave just by maintaining this position.

- Start moving the blade towards the kayak powerfully as part of the draw stroke to help move sideways off the wave.

- A second draw stroke can be used if more sideways movement is required.

EQUIPMENT CONSIDERATIONS

When enjoying rock hopping it is important to consider what equipment to use from a safety as well as performance point of view. A helmet is strongly advised when rock hopping to help prevent head injury, and it is worth considering wearing paddling gloves to protect the hands. Consider making use of a plastic sea kayak if one is available; this will prevent costly repairs of a composite kayak as well as allow greater challenges to be attempted. A kayak with a keyhole cockpit will be easier to get in and out of for the awkward landings and launching. It is worth checking to see if you can get one leg out of a kayak while afloat when choosing what kayak you may buy. A shorter set of sea kayak paddles can also help when performing tight manoeuvres around rocks.

Landing on and launching from rocks

When exploring and playing along the rocky coastlines it is not always possible to find easy landing places to have a rest, stretch the legs or sort out a problem. Here are some key considerations for landing and launching effectively in less than ideal locations.

Landing on a rocky ledge

1 + **2**   Identifying a good ledge, timing it well and being ready to step out of the kayak.

● Think tactically for any awkward landing spot; look for somewhere that will make life as easy as possible.

● Find somewhere with as much protection from the waves and swell as possible.

● Look for somewhere with some form of ledge to get out on to.

● Make sure this ledge is at the same height as the water at the top of any swell.

● Look for somewhere that, once out, gives you enough room to do whatever you need to.

● Observe at least a couple of wave sets to see how they affect the landing spot.

3 + **4**   Stepping out onto the ledge with a line clipped to the kayak.

● Time the approach to be between any sets of waves.

● Release the spray deck in readiness.

● Get one leg out of the kayak ready to get out.

- Consider having a line at the ready to clip onto the kayak as soon as you get out.

- Come in alongside the ledge with the leg out of the kayak on the same side as the ledge.

- Hold the boat with one hand and hold the ledge with the other hand.

- At the top of the swell, when the ledge is level with the kayak, stand on the ledge with the foot already out of the kayak.

- As the swell drops a bit and the kayak drops, use this to step out of the kayak onto the ledge.

- Keep one foot or the paddle loosely in the kayak so that it does not drift away, or keep hold of a pre-attached line.

Launching off a rocky ledge

 Careful timing to step and then sit in the kayak, and getting the second foot in when sat in the kayak and away from the rocks.

- Position the kayak so it is alongside the ledge.

- Stand balanced on one leg with the other resting in the cockpit.

- Have one hand on the rocks for support and the other free to help get in the kayak.

- Place the paddle somewhere where it is easy to reach or have it in the supporting hand.

- As the kayak rises to the top of a swell and is alongside the ledge, use the free hand to hold the back of the cockpit and slide the leg fully into the kayak.

- Sit down into the seat in one smooth movement.

- Keep the other foot out of the kayak and push the kayak away from the rocks.

- Once away from the rocks, put the other foot in the kayak and put on the spray deck.

- If unable to get the second leg in the kayak while afloat, then try sliding both legs into the kayak when getting in off the rocks.

Seal launch

   Timing the seal launch for when the swell comes in; seaweed covered rocks are required to minimise damage.

- If there is seaweed or smooth rocks on a launching ledge that is clear of water at the fall of the swell, consider launching off this.

- Get fully into the kayak quickly as the swell falls away and exposes the rocks which the kayak can rest on.

- If time, put on the spray deck.

- As the swell come in and picks up the kayak, push out into deep water.

- Keep leaning forwards while launching; this helps to prevent the stern catching the rocks too much.

- This technique is sometimes referred to as a seal launch.

- It is also possible to land in a similar way (a seal landing). If attempting this, extreme care should be taken as it is difficult to be sure that there are no hidden, sharp rocks that could damage a kayak. A seal landing should only be used as a last resort.

COACH'S TOP TIP

Look before you leap and develop patience. Rock gardens provide the sea kayaker with an ever-changing environment to explore; the attraction and challenge of this environment lies in the way it is affected by the ocean swell. These areas are seldom the same twice; timing and observing the effects of the swell is key.

The skills to navigate your kayak effectively lies in the accumulation of boat-handling skills, developing a unique understanding of size and volume and being able to be in the right place at the right time. Anticipating the way the wave action will form and then direct you through an obstacle is a combination of skill, technique and sometimes an element of luck. Try visualising the way in which you will be directed, the strokes necessary throughout the manoeuvre and understand the 'what ifs' involved in this process.

These intuitive skills are developed over time and, in the process, mistakes will be made. Some of these will result in chipped paddles and gel-coats, possible bruises and barnacle rash and, more often than not, in the occasional swim. Do not let these things deter you. Rock gardens are an exciting and vibrant environment where the ocean's mighty swell meets terra firma; the kayak is the only vessel that can navigate this area effectively.

Jeff Allen

Jeff has been both guiding and coaching professionally for the past 10 years. A keen expedition sea kayaker, he has journeyed by kayak for many thousands of miles. Rock gardening is one of his favourite aspects of this sport. For more information, visit *www.expeditionpaddler.com.*

OPEN CROSSINGS

To head off in a sea kayak across an expanse of open water without being able to see the next landfall is, for many a sea kayaker, the ultimate challenge. The total commitment of a crossing is a truly unique experience. Whether it is the first hour-long crossing out to an island or a seasoned kayaker's 12-hour exposed ocean crossing, the feeling of apprehension and commitment will always be there.

Regardless of whether you are a novice or a veteran open water paddler, many of the skills required to be successful when attempting these crossings are similar. Open crossings require a crucial blend of ingredients all coming together. To help understand this, the Technical, Tactical, Physiological and Psychological model I have used throughout the book is invaluable. I would suggest that, for open crossings, the most important areas to focus on would be the tactical and the psychological.

Technical considerations

When considering technical skills for open crossings, the main areas I consider are the paddling skills that will be required. Although it is fair to say that an open crossing is all about forward paddling, it is also important to consider some other technical paddling skills.

Good forward paddling is essential for the open crossings.

- Ensure your forward paddling stroke is as efficient as possible and is good enough to paddle the distance of your crossing.

- Have the ability to vary your forward paddling; this can allow different muscles to be used then rested while on a long crossing. Changing from high-angle paddling to low-angle paddling is one way of doing this, changing the cadence (stroke rate) is another.

- Ensure your forward paddling can stay consistent and efficient in a range of conditions that may be encountered on a crossing.

- It is essential to feel stable and balanced in the kayak, whether it is moving or stationary. Rests will need to be taken and, if rafting up is not the best option, being comfortably able to maintain stability is important.

- If solo, having a system to rest in rough water is important (a paddle float may be an option).

- Ensure you have the skills to deal with any rough water and swell that will be encountered.

- Launching and landing will be required, often on an exposed island or coastline; ensure you have the technical skills to do this safely.

- If with a group, rafting up will be useful. Be able to manoeuvre the kayak efficiently without wasting energy to get into rafted up position.

- If solo, self rescue skills are essential.

- In a group, self and group rescue skills need to be practised.

Tactical considerations

Without well-thought-out tactics it would be impossible to be safe, comfortable and efficient on an open crossing. Although being highly skilled is enough to keep out of trouble in many areas of sea kayaking, if good tactics are not in place on an open crossing it will be, at best, uncomfortable and hard work and, at worst, result in an encounter with Davey Jones' locker! The tactics for open crossings are all those items that take a bit of planning.

Getting the planning right is essential for the tactics of open crossings.

- Ensure the distance, navigation, tides and timings are all well researched (and checked) at home, well before the crossing.

- Decide on the upper limit of winds that you are happy with for the crossing, watch the weather closely and do not be tempted to start if the forecast is not perfect for you.

- Be patient; it will often take more than one attempt to get the right weather for a planned crossing.

- Use the ocean to help the paddling; adjust to a forward trim to gain speed going down waves, make the most of the shelter from the wind in the troughs and use the peaks of waves to see ahead.

- Choose the right group of people to go with; this is as important from a social aspect as it is from a paddling ability perspective.

- Choose the best kayak for the job: comfort, stability and speed are key considerations.

COACH'S TOP TIP

Peeing at sea is an art form and the options for females are: sitting, standing or swimming.

When sitting in the kayak there are peeing devices such as a 'shewee' or 'you go girl', both of which are ergonomically designed funnels with a spout. Take your spray deck off and then insert the device through a relief zip. Slightly lift the weight off your buttocks by leaning on the back rim of the cockpit and get the device positioned with a good seal on the skin. This will need to be held in place with one hand while the other holds a bottle over the spout. This definitely takes practise, as there is a tendency for the device to drip on retrieval. In rougher conditions, you need to be well balanced or raft up. The preferred method I have is a large cup (a 2 litre plastic bottle cut down to about a litre and slightly shaped, with gaffa tape to seal the edges around the top). I wear an oversized pair of salopettes with a large waisted spray deck so that I can lift my cag and insert the cup down the salopettes. I prefer this method when I am out by myself as you don't have to take the spray deck off and you have a free hand to balance.

You can stand up and pee, although this needs a partner to help. Raft up with your partner (with their boat positioned slightly further forward). Take off the spray deck and use your cockpit rim or partner's buoyancy aid to help stand up and balance. With one foot on their back deck and one foot just in front of your seat it is possible to pee between the boats. (This is also a handy method when on a really long crossing if it's the time of the month.)

The final method is to jump in for a swim and have a pee. Recommended only in warm water and on a warm day!

Fiona Whitehead

Fiona is a Level 5 Sea Coach and works for the Outward Bound Trust. She aspires to enable as many young people as possible to have the opportunity to experience adventures and journeys in wild places. Some of this is through having her own adventures, leading expeditions or coaching other staff to lead expeditions and adventures for young people.

- Set the kayak up so that there is room in the cockpit to stretch out legs and move a bit. Ensure the fit is also good for forward paddling.

- Good paddles make a huge difference. If your paddle length or feather can be adjusted, this will help to vary forward paddling and give flexibility.

- Drip rings on paddles are great for crossings; dry hands will generally blister and rub up less.

- Get the clothing system right as being too hot or cold will lead to fatigue. A system that allows venting and adjustment is important. I avoid cag decks or drysuits on most crossings because of this.

- If on a longer crossing you will need to go for a pee; be prepared for this and have a pee system practised and in place.

- Have all-important equipment readily available for accessing while afloat. Consider which hatches are accessible, what can go in buoyancy aid (PFD) or jacket pockets and if a deck bag or bum bag is needed. Do not rely on having anything in the cockpit; chances are it may be too rough to release a spray deck.

Good planning so all the essentials are at hand is a must.

- Have a good hydration system in place and ensure you can access easy-to-eat food while afloat.

- A GPS receiver is invaluable when on crossings; know how to use one and have spare batteries at hand.

- Emergency communications are essential, along with a means to receive updated forecasts while on the crossing. Consider the pros and cons of VHF, satellite phone, emergency locator beacons, mobile phones and flares for the crossing being undertaken.

TOP TIPS

It is obviously much easier to go for a pee at sea for us male paddlers than for our female paddling companions. That said, it is a skill worth practising before being caught short. I find the majority of paddling trousers make it awkward to pee out of when sat down – check this out before you have to go! I generally choose to either not bother with paddling trousers for crossings if the weather is good, or use a set with an elasticised waist and no braces (ensuring it is not tucked up under my spray deck waist). Alternatively, a pair of mountain waterproof trousers with a zip and fastener at the front also works well.

Trousers sorted, a handy pee bottle will be required. Take something with as wide a neck as possible, as it will be surprisingly easy to miss. When it comes to going, a friend not easily embarrassed is handy to have around since being rafted up makes a huge difference (a paddle float is a possible second option if support is required).

Releasing the spray deck is easiest, but if this is not possible consider a spray deck with a very wide waist which will allow access. For most people it is then just a matter of sorting yourself out, usually lifting your bum slightly off the seat by resting back against the cockpit rim, and peeing away. I have one friend who seems not to need a pee bottle and can go straight over the side – I am sure his seat is raised higher than most!

Having food and drink available is essential to keep the engine running.

Physiological considerations

Ensuring that there is enough fuel in the engine to complete the crossing is essential. As already indicated with the tactical considerations, making sure that the fuel is available while afloat is also essential. In addition to this, it is also important to know that the body is fit and strong enough for the job in hand. Most of the physiological considerations for open crossings will be covered in the "Physical considerations' chapter; a few specifics are listed below.

- Hydration is vital; it is all too easy to avoid drinking if water is not easily available or if trying to avoid going for a pee.

- Keep drinking little and often throughout a crossing. The chances are this will not necessitate extra pee stops, but if it does then it will still have been worth it from an energy point of view.

- Eat well and appropriately before the crossing, and have all the correct energy sources of food available to hand while afloat.

- Use food and drink that you have tried and tested; this is not the place to discover that a certain product makes you nauseous.

- Be organised with food, drink and rest stops when on a crossing; it is all too easy to just keep paddling until overtired, by which time it is too late to take on food and rest.

- I would recommend paddling for 50–55 minutes and resting for 5–10 minutes. Keeping this in hour blocks also makes the tidal planning and timing easier.

- While resting, take the time to gently relax and stretch the back, shoulders and legs.

- Look after your body when afloat; think about sun cream, lip salve, sun hat, sunglasses, etc.

- Do everything possible to avoid rubs and blisters; make sure the kit you use is tried and tested.

- Keeping hands as dry as possible can help prevent rubs and blisters. If blisters start on hands however, tape them up before they get too bad. Electrical tape works well for this.

- If rubs start under armpits, then Sudocrem® is a lifesaver. Vaseline® (petroleum jelly) can also be used.

Starting off on an open crossing is all about mind over matter.

Psychological considerations

As already indicated in the introduction, open crossings are as much a mind game as anything else. With a considered psychological approach, even the most committing of open crossings can become a positive and successful adventure. There is a saying that is used by fast jet pilots: "never take the body where the mind has not been before". This could not be truer for open crossings, and the 'Psychological considerations' chapter will go into this in greater depth. There are a few key points for the paddler taking on an open crossing however, listed in the following.

- The unknowns are usually the main psychological constraints, so the key is to get rid of as many of them as possible.

- The length of time in the kayak without being able to land is often a key worry when embarking on an open crossing. To cope with this ensure you have spent at least as much time without getting out of a boat prior to the crossing, but on a coastal journey that is escapable if required.

COACH'S TOP TIPS

I learnt to sea kayak in the Channel Islands. Small islands, strong tidal streams, summer fog and committing crossings were the norm.

It is surprising how your own fears and insecurity can turn a pleasant paddle into a scary crossing. The trick is to build up your experience gradually and so create a 'psychological reserve'. Start with short crossings to large targets that are reassuringly visible. Only attempt your early crossings in settled weather and good visibility. When you start paddling out to small targets, make sure that you are fit enough to paddle twice the distance envisaged. That way, if you completely blow it you can paddle back to the mainland and, more importantly, you know you can.

Above all, remember that there is always a 'Plan B' (even if you haven't thought of it yet)! In the days before GPS, a few friends and I were crossing from Jersey to the relatively small island of Sark. About halfway across, the wind died and thick fog developed. Radiating a confidence I didn't necessarily feel, I paddled on our bearing and trusted my carefully calculated tidal vectors. When the anticipated crossing time had elapsed and there was still no sign of land, I announced that we would paddle for another 15 minutes. If there was still no sign of land after that, we would go for Plan B. Five minutes later, there was a collective sigh of relief as we heard the bell of the buoy that is just outside the tiny harbour.

Over a pint that evening I was asked what Plan B was. Simple! The tide would have been running north for another couple of hours, making an immediate return to Jersey impossible. On the plus side, there was no wind. We would therefore conserve energy and drift with the tide for two hours to the north and, after it turned, for two hours to the south. If the fog had lifted by then, we would go to nearby Sark. If it hadn't, we would paddle back with the tide to the much larger target of Jersey. No problem!

Franco Ferrero

- Being able to cope with the conditions is another worry; prior to the crossing get out in worse conditions than the forecast would ever throw up on your crossing, but in a safe escapable environment. That way you will know you can deal with any conditions that may arise.

- Build up the distance of crossings gradually; start with an hour, then maybe two and so on. Unknowns then become manageable.

- Trust your equipment and be totally familiar with it and the spares being carried. Again, get rid of any unknowns in terms of how gear may or may not perform.

- Prior to setting off, find a safe spot and practise anything that may be needed on the crossing that you have not done before. Going for a pee, eating, drinking and resting while afloat are all examples of this.

- Plan the trip, then plan it again, then check it and then check it again. Finally, get someone else to plan it independently and compare your results. If you know what to expect and are prepared for the job, it is half done.

- Being totally at ease with those around you (or not in the solo case) is essential. Trusting yourself and your fellow paddlers is fundamental for maximum confidence.

PERFORMER'S TOP TIP

In the grand scheme of things, such a small number of serious crossings have been done that there is no single authority on the subject and no textbook way of doing things. You will learn something new every time you venture out because the dangers always vary. In the Channel it's shipping, the Minch is renowned for steep vicious waves, and the Irish Sea and Pentland Firth have currents that have to be seen to be believed. Your kayak, the weather, water temperature and wildlife are a few additional factors that might determine how successful/safe you are.

My first tip is obvious: know exactly what you are taking on. Have sleepless nights working out what might go wrong and then develop and test systems and kit to deal with the worst. For the first time in 40 years of paddling, Mike Berwick came out of his boat this year. He seldom needs to roll and had never needed a self rescue. He was shocked at how difficult it was and humiliated by the fact that he couldn't do it. Practise is everything.

One factor that never changes is the need to be organised. Everything you need has to be accessible. Prioritise, colour code all your bags and have a home for each bit of kit. If all team members pack their boats in the same way, this can save hours on a long trip and save lives when things go wrong.

Discipline is another must. Establish the routine you need and stick to it. Five minutes rest an hour is generally enough to reorganise, refuel and recover, but five easily turns to ten if there is no one focused on the clock. Now your troubles really start as you miss tide changes, weather windows and possibly your ultimate goal.

If paddling in excess of ten hours, someone in the group will at some point feel grim. You have to have the strength to stay behind them. Your turn for misery will come, and only then can you appreciate the psychological benefits of leading and navigating. It may not always be fun, but enjoy what is essentially a unique experience.

I recommend having with you: a satellite phone (pricy but priceless); a kayak which has a skeg or rudder; a Blizzard heat pad; and a Reed kayak tent (proven lifesaver). Rhythmical paddling is the key to easy distance, whichever technique you use make sure it works in all conditions. Finally, ensure that you can paddle left- or right-handed in case of tendon inflammation.

Patrick Winterton

Patrick has spent the last six years pushing his limits of open sea crossings. His latest include a 2200 km voyage retracing the route of St Brendan 'the Navigator' and the first kayak expedition to make the 3-day crossing from Scotland to the Faroe Islands. His presentations combine stunning footage and entertaining anecdotes that may tempt you to venture further out to sea. Contact Patrick via pww@patrickwinterton.com.

ROLLING

Many sea kayakers spend a lifetime exploring amazing coastlines happy to rely on their balance and, in the rare event of a capsize, the ability of their friends to rescue them. As well as being the quickest rescue technique out there (and therefore the safest), being able to roll gives you the confidence to take paddling performance to another level. Whether practising calm water edging or trying to turn a kayak on a steep wave face, the simple knowledge that if it goes wrong you can just roll up is often all that is needed to perfect the manoeuvre. The majority of paddlers will gain huge confidence in being able to roll in any conditions, and this will get them comfortable in the rough water environment. This ability to be relaxed in the environment is at the heart of all the skills in the book so, if you are to develop your rough water skills, rolling is crucial.

The roll

There are many different types of roll out there and they all have their advantages and disadvantages; at the end of the day, if it works it can't be too far away from being pretty good. When considering the roll you have or learning to be able to roll, there are a few key features that must be part of the roll for it to be appropriate on the sea.

- The roll must be safe and have no chance of damaging shoulders through overextension or backs from too much force and rotation.

- The roll must leave you in a 'ready to paddle' position; if it does not, then another capsize will be sure to follow.

- The roll must be performed without having to move hands on your paddle or overly set up. There may not be time for this in rough water and, if hands are moved, the 'ready to paddle' position will not be there once upright.

- The roll needs to be developed to the point where you no longer have to think about it, preferably on both sides.

If you have a roll that ticks all the above boxes, great! If not, then consider adapting your roll so that it does. If it helps, here is my preferred way of rolling. It starts with a sweep roll to get the sea kayak starting to roll, then finishes with the 'C-to-C' roll to finish the job.

1 + 2 The set-up position where the upper body forms a 'C' shape towards the paddle.

- Ensure that you are relaxed at the hips.

- Be patient; wait for the boat to settle fully upside down.

- Reach over as far as possible with your hands so that the front paddle blade is out of the water.

- Develop the feel of when the front blade is out of the water.

- Ensure that the head is forward and positioned as close as possible towards the side of the knee.

- Keep the rear hand relaxed and close to the side of the kayak.

- The upper body should be forming a 'C' shape towards the paddle (on the left side of the paddler's body in the photo).

3 + 4 Sweeping the blade out to the side, ensuring the blade is not pulled downwards.

- Start sweeping the blade away from the side of the kayak.

- Ensure that the blade is angled very slightly to help prevent it from diving too much.

- Do not pull down on the blade, but focus on moving it out and away from the kayak.

- Gentle pressure should be felt on the blade.

- As the blade starts to sweep out, start to gently lift the knee that is on the same side as the front hand on the paddle (if right hand is at the front, then lift the right knee, as in the photo).

- Allow the hips to stay relaxed.

- Relax the opposite knee so it drops towards the hull of the kayak; this helps the kayak to start rolling.

- Keep the rear hand out of the water and close to the side of the kayak; the elbow should remain tucked in to the body.

- Start to finish the sweep when the blade is coming close to 90° to the kayak.

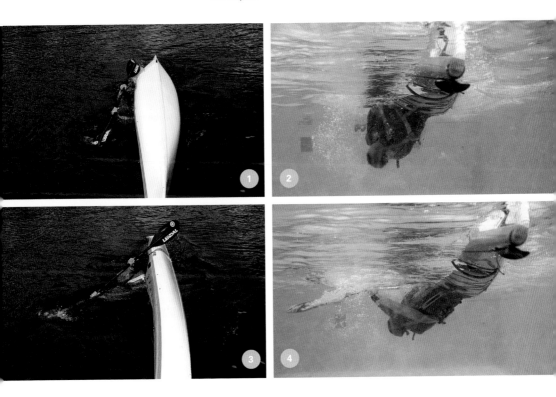

⑤ + ⑥ With the blade at about 90°, start to pull down on it while lifting the knee and forming a 'C' shape on the opposite side to the set-up.

- As the blade comes towards 90° to the kayak, start to gently increase the downward pressure on the blade.

- As this happens, increase the pressure on the knee to start rolling the kayak upright.

- While this knee is driving upwards, stay relaxed in the hips and the opposite knee so that the kayak rolls separately to the upper body.

- Having formed a 'C' shape with the upper body in the set-up (to the left), by gently pulling on the blade and driving the knee upwards a 'C' shape should now be formed on the opposite side of the body (i.e. to the right of the paddler's body).

⑦ + ⑧ As the body moves into the 'C' shape, ensure that the head is the last thing to come out of the water.

- Ensure that the boat moves first with the knee, then allow the body to move into the 'C' shape to assist this. The head comes out of the water after the body as the boat turns upright.

- By combining the knee lift, gentle pressure on the blade and body movement in moving from the 'C-to-C' shape, the roll will be possible.

- Ensure that the head stays relaxed and is the last thing to come out of the water when the kayak in upright.

- With good use of the 'C-to-C' movement, the blade should not have dived too deep in the water.

⑨ + ⑩ As the kayak starts to become upright move the blade and body forward into a stable position.

- When the kayak is upright it is important to immediately adopt a ready-to-paddle position.

- Convert the end of the roll into a brace position to help with this, providing instant stability.

- If the roll is finished slightly back, or the paddle needs to be moved to get into a forward paddling position, move the brace across the surface of the water into this position.

- Again this will provide support and stability while getting into a forward paddling position.

ENVIRONMENTAL CONSIDERATIONS

Having a basic bombproof roll such as the one described above is an essential firm foundation. However, the more different types of roll you can perform, the more able you will be to cope with different conditions. In powerful surf for example, you may find yourself pinned to the back deck as you capsize. If you can start the roll from this position it saves a lot of time, effort and oxygen getting into the set–up position.

Rough water rolling considerations

Being able to roll in the calm water is one thing, being able to roll where it counts in the rough water is another. If the roll is bombproof on the calm water then it will work on the rough, so getting well practised on calm water is the first step. The roll needs to become second nature on calm water, so that there is complete confidence it will work with very little thought required. If this is the case, then the only thing that will usually stop it working in the rough is the paddler not being relaxed and the pressure of the situation changing the roll. A few considerations for rolling in rough water are listed below.

Being able to roll when it counts is essential.

- Ensure there is complete confidence when rolling in calm water; that way you know you will be able to roll even though it is rough.

- Develop confidence in the rough water by taking progressive learning steps in the environment.

- Use the above to ensure that when practising or needing to roll you can stay as relaxed as possible.

- The kayak will often take longer to fully settle upside down in rough water; be patient and wait for this to happen.

- If the kayak does not settle upside down on one side, change to a roll on the other side if you can.

- In strong side winds the kayak may be prevented from settling upside down; in this case, changing the rolling side may be essential.

- If you have a choice, capsize downwind to help with the above.

- Ensure that the roll is finished in the bracing and ready-to-paddle position; this will help prevent a further capsize in rough conditions.

- If the first roll does not succeed, this may be due to unlucky timing and being hit by a wave or wind just as you are trying to get fully upright.

- If the above happens, try to get a breath of air, relax and attempt the roll again; you know that your rolling technique works.

- If you know you are caught in a breaking wave or other feature that will disappear, wait until it becomes calmer before attempting to roll.

- Sometimes a wave or wind can actually help the roll; again, finishing on a brace will prevent any surprisingly easy rolls ending up in another capsize.

- Keep the amount of kit on the deck of the kayak to a minimum; this will just get in the way and cause drag in the roll.

- If all attempts are repeatedly failing, consider moving the hands down the paddle shaft to extend the paddle for increased leverage.

Troubleshooting

There is no doubt about it: rolling is one of the most challenging kayaking skills that we attempt to learn. For many of us, it will be a long learning journey with many frustrations along the way. To be able to start in a swimming pool and progress into other environments with the help of some coaching is the ideal, and even with this it could still take a while to develop that bombproof roll. For most students learning to roll, there are many common errors which prevent success.

COACH'S TOP TIP

To develop your Eskimo roll in rough water, you have to make the experience 'playful' and fun. We get uptight if we take rolling too seriously, and we all know how too much stress can undermine our performance! Rolling in more challenging conditions is about three things: confidence, orientation and coordination.

Confidence: in your own ability; the more relaxed you are the less air you consume.

Orientation: where you are and how you can get your paddle into a position to roll; it doesn't have to be textbook perfect, just good enough to kick-start the movement!

Coordination: the more harmonious the movement between body, boat and blade, the less effort is required for a successful roll (particularly important when fatigued).

Surf is a fantastic, dynamic environment to play in and is ideal for developing all those skills that underpin the ability to roll (particularly when conditions challenge you). The break doesn't need to be huge; even in small waves the breaking water is great for developing skills such as balance, edge awareness, agility, timing, understanding of the boat, impact of equipment on movement, etc. Use surf to develop that all-important self-confidence. Spending time in a dynamic environment such as surf will engage you both mentally and physically, setting you well on the path to a bombproof roll.

Do not lose sight of the fun aspect; its all a game after all.

Oisin Hallissey

Oisin is Head of Canoeing at Tollymore, Northern Ireland's National Outdoor Centre. He is a Level 5 Sea Coach and loves to get away to remote parts of the world as well as share his experience and knowledge with those attending courses. Check out courses at *www.tollymore.com* or email Oisin at oisinhallissey@tollymore.com.

- The roll will only work if the 'C' shape is achieved so that the head is the last thing out of the water.

- To help with the above, think about starting the roll with the boat first, the body second and the head last.

- There has to be an upper and lower body separation for the 'C' shape to happen; stay relaxed at the hips for this to be achieved.

- To start the sweep, the blade must be on the surface of the water. Get the feel of when this happens by pushing it to the surface then tapping it on the surface before attempting to roll.

- Set the angle of the blade so it gives support by skimming across the surface. If the angle is too small it will dive; if too great it will drag in the water.

- Getting the sweeping motion of the blade is key, as this prevents the blade from diving down.

- With the above, think about moving the blade away from the boat as opposed to pulling down on the blade.

- Try not to punch up with the top hand; this can lead to injury (remember the safety box) and makes the sweeping blade dive.

- Keep the hand furthest away from the rolling blade relaxed and with the elbow tucked in, as if you were holding a newspaper under the arm.

- Keep constant driving pressure on the knee that is helping roll the kayak upright.

TOP TIPS

The head coming up too early is so often the key error which prevents a successful roll. To help with this, try to focus on looking towards the bottom of the sea as you roll up. While doing this, imagine you are (or actually do if you have enough air) blowing bubbles in the water. Try to blow these bubbles for as long as possible until the boat is upright, this ensures the head comes up last in a good position. Another way to think about it is to imagine that someone has glued your ear to the shoulder that is nearest the rolling blade as you are rolling up. With this ear glued to the shoulder, focus on looking at the rolling blade. Again, this will help with the head position.

- Try not to finish the roll too far back; this overextends the arm and could result in injury.

- With the above, it will also prevent the 'C' shape and the hips and knee to help finish the roll.

- If you have less flexibility you will sometimes find that finishing further back in the roll is required; keep this to a minimum and ensure there is no overextending of the arms.

PHYSICAL CONSIDERATIONS

No matter how technically competent in a kayak you are, long trips will be beyond your capabilities if you do not have the muscular endurance required. Even if you are fully prepared and as fit as you have ever been, if you do not get the food right on an expedition you will have insufficient fuel in the engine and will grind to a halt. Underlying everything that is covered in this book is a need to be physically aware of what is going to be required of your body and how best to prepare it. In this chapter we look at some of the key considerations for the sea paddler; it is not an in-depth look at physiology, but a way of signposting areas you may wish to look into further.

Diet

"YOU ARE WHAT YOU EAT"

In my opinion, this is fundamental to everything we want to do in paddling. On every expedition I have ever been on, the biggest topic of conversation is food. Get it right and there is energy for any situation that may have to be dealt with and harmony among the team; good food leads to happy paddlers! Get it wrong and there is no energy to survive comfortably; people struggle, morale plummets, things go wrong and, without a doubt, the expedition will not be remembered as a success. On an early expedition when we were away for two months I miscalculated and ran out of food with a week to go. It was a mistake I made once and paid the price. Food is now the number one priority on all expeditions and trips I put together. It does not have to be fancy food, but it does need to provide the energy required along with having variety for morale and that feel-good factor. A balanced diet is essential, so understanding some of the key nutrients that make up our diet and how they can affect us in our paddling will help get the most from a paddling diet. A few considerations for planning your food can be found below.

Choosing the right expedition food is essential.

Nutritional value

Whether an afternoon playing on a tidal race or a month-long expedition, it is vital to have the correct amount of food which delivers the energy when you need. The daily energy requirements for an average lifestyle are 2000–2500kcal for women and 2500–3000kcal for men. When going out for a day's paddling, about 30% more than this will be needed on average to be able to perform well. When away on extended expeditions, I tend to work out the rations to be in the region of 3500–4500kcal per day. In addition to this, you need to consider the make-up of this food and when to eat it. This doesn't just apply to the planned food on expedition, but also the junk food that may be consumed while travelling to a weekend paddling destination and how this could affect paddling performance and energy levels.

TOP TIPS

Expedition food: aim to eat 3500–4500kcal per day on a demanding expedition. In the evening and morning, try to ensure the majority of food is made up of complex carbohydrates and fats. Have plenty of simple carbohydrates (sugar-based foods) easily available during the day. Variety is essential for morale; plan the menu around this as well as nutrition.

Day trip food: aim to eat about 2500–3500kcal during the day (more if it is a big demanding day). Have a good breakfast with complex carbohydrates, plenty of simple carbohydrates at hand during the day, then when landed have a mix of simple and complex carbohydrates.

Carbohydrates

These are the body's major energy source and the foods we need to be most aware of as paddlers, to keep the engine firing on all six cylinders. They are generally split into two types referred to as simple and complex carbohydrates. For us as paddlers, we may come to know them more easily as quick and slow carbs. Understanding these will help get the balance right when sorting out food for our afternoons playing on the tidal races or on expeditions.

Simple or quick carbs are the foods that give us that quick hit of energy, as they are readily absorbed into the blood stream and can act quickly once there. They are usually sugar based and are the equivalent of throwing some kindling on the fire to get it burning quickly. We have all been out on the sea and had that energy low; when this happens, we need some quick carbs to get us going again. Instead of waiting for that energy low to happen, it is best to get to know your body and snack regularly on quick carbs to maintain constant energy during the exercise period. Examples of quick carbs are: dried fruits, cereal bars, chocolate bars, sugary drinks or (the champion of all foods in my opinion) jelly babies! While out paddling, ensure you have plenty of this type of food readily at hand and accessible while afloat.

Complex or slow carbs are at the heart of expedition food and essential to keep the body's energy systems constantly ready. Energy from the food is released slowly into the blood stream in a sustainable manner; the slow carbs are the equivalent of loading the fire up with coal so that it keeps burning all night. When planning our paddling diet we need to ensure that evening meals and breakfasts have a good amount of slow carbs and that these make up the majority of our planned kilocalorie intake. Examples of slow carbs include: pasta, potatoes, some cereals (porridge or muesli) and bread. When there is a choice of brown or white (e.g. bread or pasta), then white is more refined and releases energy quicker.

It is worth considering what to eat at lunch and trying to get a mix of complex and simple carbs. Oatcakes, brown bread and pasta are good to have from a complex carb point of view. If these sit too heavily in the stomach, consider white bread or wraps as these will release energy quicker into the blood stream.

Top left: choose camp food with plenty of slow carbs.
Top right: when snacking afloat, fast-acting carbs are needed.

Fats

Fats provide highly concentrated stores of energy within the body. Although they do not provide energy as readily as carbohydrates, they do contain about twice as much energy pound for pound. They can therefore be good for expeditions as they are lighter to carry, but should not be eaten at breakfast or lunch due to them being slow to digest. They are the body's natural emergency food as well as insulation against the cold, so clearly for us sea paddlers they have some advantages. When paddling, fat may be burned for energy as well as carbohydrates as it can be a low-intensity form of exercise. Paddlers with low fat content on long expeditions may find they deplete their body's fat stores and should consider this in their diet planning. Fats can be found in animals and plants and are categorised as either saturated (e.g. dairy products, red meat, chicken and chocolate) or unsaturated (e.g. fish, peanuts and olive oil). It is generally considered that unsaturated fats are better for you.

TOP TIPS

When heading away on expedition, ensure that the food is planned well in advance. Consider either pre-packing it or at least knowing the amounts you need to get the correct amount of calories. I will often pre-pack porridge for breakfast; it gives the best calories for weight and space you can get. I will weigh out a breakfast-sized portion then add some dried milk, sugar, cinnamon and perhaps sultanas or dried apples. This will be in a bag ready to go ensuring space is saved, life is simple for cooking and the correct amount of fuel gets into the boiler. When planning expedition food, some examples of single portions include: 50g of porridge oats; 110g of rice; and 125g of pasta.

In the perfect world good food should never be too far away!

Proteins

These provide the basis for building and repairing muscles and other tissues within the body. When out sea kayaking, it is almost inevitable that muscles and other body tissues will be damaged; providing the body with the means to repair these is essential. The recommended daily intake of protein is 15% of the total daily calories; this is fine for paddlers when on day trips or expeditions. It is important to get proteins from a variety of sources as the complete protein is made up of 20 amino acids which are the key building blocks for the muscles and tissues. Meats, fish, eggs and dairy products are good sources for complete proteins. Rice, pulses and beans are also good sources of protein, but don't contain the complete range of amino acids; an appropriately balanced diet is necessary for this.

Minerals and vitamins

These are essential elements of a diet and assist in cell function and chemical reactions to promote growth and maintain health. If a balanced diet is followed as advised, then an appropriate amount of minerals and vitamins will normally be eaten. If away on extended expeditions or suffering from specific health conditions, it may be worth considering mineral or vitamin supplements.

COACH'S TIP

When about to commence any journey or new adventure it is important that we are performing at our optimum in order to get the most from our paddling. This can be compromised if we have not prepared ourselves through eating, drinking and preparing ourselves physically and psychologically. Even if these elements of our preparation are simply crammed into the day before, neglecting them has the potential to hamper an amazing paddling experience.

During the paddle monitor change in behaviour. If you or others start to experience what I call the 'hangries' (where you get snappy or go very quiet), your body is hungry for food. Alternatively, check for bags forming under your eyes (another telltale sign). In my

experience, the best way of checking if our body is ready is through our wee (hydration) and poo (food intake). If you achieve the perfect poo, you know you are ready to take on whatever challenge awaits.

Dr Gilly Mara

Gilly is a lecturer in elite sports performance and a freelance sports consultant and coach educator. She has competed internationally at wild water racing and has completed the Devizes to Westminster in under 20 hours in the non-stop women's K2 class.

Hydration

Our bodies are made up of about 60–80% water and only oxygen is more important than water for us to survive. As sea paddlers, it is possibly the area we neglect most when it comes to providing our body with what it needs to function at an optimal level. The challenges of going for a pee while afloat, having water easy to drink in rough conditions or the weight of carrying enough water when it is not readily available from streams are a few examples of why we often suffer from dehydration on a paddling trip. As soon as the body becomes at all dehydrated, fatigue and performance deterioration will follow; on any type of paddling trip the consequences of this are obvious.

Keeping hydrated is essential.

It is recommended that about 2–3 litres of water should be taken on board every day. The amount of water required will vary with the person, the activity and the environment; being able to identify the first signs of dehydration are therefore important. If it is hot or humid and sweating is occurring, clearly more water will be required to hydrate. Monitor the colour of your urine; this should be straw coloured and not dark yellow and, on average, you should be going every 2–4 hours where possible. Be aware of headaches or fatigue as this could also be linked to dehydration. It therefore cannot be emphasised enough: as a sea paddler we must drink plenty of fluids throughout the day.

These fluids could simply be water; alternatively, sports drinks can be considered as hydration as well as an energy source. Unfortunately, alcohol will not help the hydration process and care needs to be taken that it is not drunk at the expense of water. It will actually have a dehydrating effect as well as interfering with normal blood sugar levels. Although high in calories, it is a poor source of carbohydrates and is of little help for energy levels. I would suggest that the benefits of the whisky around the campfire are purely psychological as opposed to physical!

Whisky may be good for the soul but it is not good for hydration.

Key to ensuring you stay hydrated is being organised and having systems in place that allow you to have a drink at any time during the day, whatever the conditions. Drink plenty before going afloat. It takes two hours for water to clear the system, so fully hydrate all evening and through the night. Try to avoid over-hydrating at breakfast if you want to avoid extra pee stops when afloat. Have plans in place to stop regularly for a pee either on land or afloat. Having the means to carry plenty of water within the kayak in water containers is also essential so that, even if there are no streams available when landing, lack of water is not a problem. Getting into the habit of keeping these containers full of water by making use of any streams etc. during the day is important, as well as knowing how much water is required. It is this planning that helps prevent dehydration and, in turn, ensures performance and energy. On an expedition, my motto is hydrate or die!

TOP TIPS

Try to drink regularly while paddling, with the aim of keeping up with the body's fluid loss. A bladder pack as part of the buoyancy aid is a great way to do this as it can be used easily in all conditions while afloat. A drinks bottle on the deck also works well; although it is not as convenient to drink out of as a bladder pack, it has the advantage of letting you see how much water is left in it. Get into the habit of filling any drinks bottle or bladder pack whenever you are off the water; this ensures they are always full and ready to use.

Fitness

There is no denying the fact that the fitter and stronger you are, the better you will be able to paddle. If good technique and tactics are combined with increased fitness, then a sea paddler will be able to paddle longer and more effectively. That said, sea kayaking is not an activity where fitness training is essential; for many, a lifetime of paddling can be enjoyed with no training (other than paddling regularly) ever done or even considered. If you are happy to get out paddling and do as much as you feel like on the day, then training is not a consideration. However, if you have an open crossing or expedition planned which is further than you have ever attempted before, including some training in your preparation could have a positive effect on success. Combined with being fit enough for the planned paddle is also the need to prevent injuries; some key fitness principles should be considered by all paddlers when it comes to this.

Left: jogging is always a good warm-up.
Right: remember to warm up the shoulders and arms.

Warm up and warm down

If you have been sat in the car for a few hours driving to a destination or have just packed the kayak with the camping gear on a cold morning, the body is in for a shock when it has to pick up and lift the kayak or take those first few strokes. It is at this time, when the body's muscles are not ready for what they are being asked to do, that tweaks happen and injuries can follow. Help the body out by preparing it for what it is about to be subjected to by getting the muscles all warmed up and the various joints gently mobilised.

On land, some fast walking and general movement of the legs, hips, shoulders and arms all help to get them warm and mobilised. Stretching is not recommended at this stage, as the idea is to purely warm up and prepare the muscles for the range of movement they are about to be used in and no more. When on water, start slowly and build up the speed, force and range of movement.

Simple mobilisation and warm-up exercises can be done while sat in the kayak waiting for others before heading off.

When stepping out of the kayak at the end of the day, we have all hobbled up the beach as if decades older. This is another key time to consider preparing the muscles for the range of movement they will be required to perform on terra firma, as well as warming down. Similar exercises to the warm-up will work well. In addition to this, it is worth considering some gentle stretching at this stage; this will help the muscles that have been used all day along with promoting future flexibility. Post-activity is a good time to stretch and, if time allows, it is well worth considering. When stretching be careful never to overdo it; only stretch in a range that is comfortable. At the limit of this range look to hold the stretch in a static position for about 15 seconds, breathing as you do so. If you are suffering from an injury, consider consulting a physiotherapist for help on what warm-ups/downs and stretching could assist for future paddling.

Stretching once off the water at the end of the day.

Core strength

Posture is key to be able to perform efficient and effective strokes. In addition to this, good posture is essential to prevent possible injuries. If you have got off the water with lower backache or tight shoulders, poor posture is often the route cause of this. In time, this will of course lead to injury.

Core strength is essential for good posture and to transfer power from the blade through the body and into the boat. Without this core strength, poor posture and lack of power will mean it is impossible to paddle effectively. If you only consider one form of training for paddling, this should

Left: core strength is essential for good posture. Right: Swiss fit ball, a great way to develop core strength.

be core strength. It is guaranteed to improve performance and, more importantly, help prevent future injuries (therefore providing a lifetime of paddling enjoyment). In its simplest form, core strength training could just take the form of getting into the habit of engaging the stomach's core muscles when doing everything. That could be sat at the computer, driving the car or walking the dog, as long as the body's posture is being maintained through the core as opposed to through the back. To train and develop the core further will most definitely lead to increased benefits; consider getting some training in the likes of the Swiss fit ball, pilates or yoga for this.

Left: Just get out paddling – lots! Right: Training on a paddling machine.

Muscular endurance

This is the ability of the muscles to repeatedly contract for a long period of time. For the sea kayaker, the muscles could be in use from anything from 1 to 24 hours in a single trip. In addition, there may only be a limited resting time before it starts all over again (an expedition may continue for many weeks or months). From a physical training point of view, muscular endurance is therefore the main area to focus on alongside core strength. With good muscular endurance there is less chance of injury, as the body is not being put in an overload situation.

There are a variety of ways to develop muscular endurance; simply getting out kayaking more often will be enough. The key thing is to ensure that whatever you do helps to develop the relevant muscles (e.g. for paddling into wind or with a heavy kayak). When deciding what training to do remember that variety is good; go for something you find enjoyable and which fits easily into daily life.

Long slow distance training

Get out paddling for longer distances, but ensuring that the intensity is low and the heart rate is steady at 60–70% of maximum. Start with a very manageable distance and slowly build this up. If you are heading off on a trip and expecting to be paddling a certain daily distance, then use this as the distance to build up to and become comfortable at.

Interval training

Mix up the rate and intensity of the paddling during the training session. Have periods on long slow distance rate, but also include periods of faster speed, higher intensity or greater resistance. To get increased resistance, paddle with a heavier-laden kayak, tow something or clip a bungee which passes under the hull of the kayak to the deck lines. Push the heart rate up into the training zone (about 60–85% of maximum) for periods of anything from 30 seconds to 5 minutes.

Pyramid training

Start at a slow speed over a short distance then slowly increase the speed and distance. Once the maximum is reached, then reverse the process to repeat the stages until back at the starting speed and distance. Slowly build up the pyramid by increasing the maximum speed and distance. For example, you could paddle for 5 minutes at slow pace, 10 minutes at moderate pace and 15 minutes at faster pace, then 10 at moderate pace finishing with 5 at slow pace. The times could be increased once this becomes comfortable.

Circuit training

This takes place in a gym and uses a variety of stations to carry out specific muscular endurance exercises. These exercises can be tailored to meet the needs of the sea kayaker. This is a useful form of training in the winter months, or if time is a limiting factor.

Cross training

Get out and take part in different activities that rely on muscular endurance. This could be rowing, mountain biking, running, swimming or cross-country skiing, for example. This is useful from the point of view of variety and interest, as well as keeping you active at certain times of the year when sea kayaking may not be as accessible.

Mountain biking: great cross training when you can't get out on the sea.

Aerobic capacity

Sea kayaking is generally a moderate-to-low intensity exercise that predominantly uses oxygen as its fuel. An efficient system using the lungs and heart to get that fuel in and around the body to the muscles is therefore important. It is this ability to get the oxygen around the body that is known as aerobic capacity. With a reasonable general level of fitness, most sea kayakers will have more than enough aerobic capacity for what they do; sea kayaking is certainly not usually a highly aerobic sport.

By just getting out paddling or working on muscular endurance, the aerobic capacity of the body will develop to meet the needs of the paddler. If is felt that aerobic capacity needs to be developed and it is not possible to go kayaking, then jogging, biking or swimming are all good to develop aerobic capacity. When working on aerobic capacity, ensure that the heart rate is less than 80% of the maximum.

COACH'S TOP TIP

In my experience sea kayakers are especially poor at physical training. On longer, more arduous, trips, this can lead to real issues when conditions become difficult and there is a need to work at higher intensities. Performers in most sports will take part in sessions designed specifically to enhance their capacity to perform sport-specific work, but most sea kayakers think that just going for a paddle will achieve this. I'm afraid it won't.

If we want our bodies to improve, then we have to systematically overload them with a particular and specific purpose in mind. For example, if we want to improve our top boat speed, then a long slow paddle will not have much of an effect in achieving this. If we want to be able to move our boat easily when it is heavily laden or sprint out through a lull in the surf, we need to design training activities that make this adaptation happen. This is actually not that difficult; simply decide which attribute you need to enhance and then design an activity that exaggerates that element.

For example, to become more comfortable paddling at 4 knots then we should do short repeated intervals of paddling at 4.5 knots. This approach means completing hard drills on an easy piece of water that we would normally be comfortable on, but this is the correct way to get faster. Paddling slowly over a long distance will simply train you to be good at going slow. Next time you are preparing for a trip, ask yourself are you really preparing yourself or just going to practise what you can already do?

Chris Hodgson

Chris is a Level 5 Sea Coach and senior lecturer at the University of Chichester where he teaches Adventure Education and PE, specialising in sports performance and psychobiology. In 1999 he was part of an attempt to make an unsupported circumnavigation of Bylot Island, one of the largest uninhabited islands in the world which lies off the northern end of Baffin Island in the Nunavut Territory of Canada.

With the right food and fitness there is a world of paddling possibilities.

Power, speed and strength

When looking at fitness training for any sport, power, speed and strength all need to be considered in addition to muscular endurance and aerobic capacity. Depending on the sport, either all of the fitness components will be required in equal measure or some will be of greater importance than others.

Having appropriate power for certain manoeuvres on a windy day or on a surf wave is important to consider along with muscular endurance. When working hard to catch a wave or maintain a ferry glide, then strength may also become more important. When considering what you are going to do and how you are going to train (whether kayak, gym or cross training), ensure that strength and endurance are considered. As more specific training needs become evident (e.g. power for surfing or endurance for a long-distance open crossing) then the gym may become the preferred option. This should always be done with appropriate training and instruction and, of course, in addition to simply getting out paddling.

PSYCHOLOGICAL CONSIDERATIONS

A number of years ago I was out paddling with a good friend who was a much better paddler than myself. While paddling along, I was asking various questions to try to learn how to improve my performance. The answer that came back has stuck with me ever since and is at the heart of this chapter: "if you didn't think about it so much, you could be really good".

For the majority of us, the single biggest inhibitor to learning and maximising performance is ourselves. This is rarely our physical ability, but our actual belief in what we should or should not be able to do. What turns a good performer into a great performer is most likely to be that belief in themselves; to that end, an individual's psychology has got to be at the heart of learning and performance. To start learning the skills in this book and become confident in the rough water environment, having the ability to ensure that our mind is helping and not hindering the situation is essential. Different responses and coping strategies when facing certain situations are evident from one paddler to another. This chapter looks at some key psychological principles to help with this; when looking at these principles consider the following performance equation (Woodhouse, 2010) which shows how psychology has the power to increase or decrease performance:

PERFORMANCE = POTENTIAL +/- PSYCHOLOGY

Arousal

That dry mouth feeling, butterflies in the stomach or a heart beating faster than it should be: we have all been there. The question is what happened next? Were these feelings harnessed and controlled so that they led to a perfect performance, or did they distract and undermine confidence so that they led to poor performance and a swim?

Arousal is the degree of activation of the body that could range from deep sleep to extreme excitement; the symptoms above are anxiety signs that indicate a potential over-arousal. There are many arousal theories, but they all share the common factor that everyone has an optimal level of arousal for performance. Any levels significantly higher or lower than this will lead to a lower level of performance.

As paddlers, we need to recognise when we are under- or over-aroused and use this knowledge to identify our optimal state of arousal for paddling in challenging conditions. We need to have ways that can accordingly increase or decrease arousal levels, and which work at an individual level. In the most challenging of conditions, identifying when over-arousal is happening is essential. The catastrophe model of arousal/performance depicted below highlights how, after a small drop in performance due to over-arousal, there can then be a sudden complete crash in performance that will then take time to address. Out on the open ocean, it is clear how disastrous this could be.

Within the rest of this chapter, the key theme is to look at ways in which to manage arousal and therefore maintain an optimum level. Some refer to this as being in a 'peak flow' state of mind.

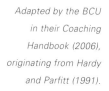

Adapted by the BCU in their Coaching Handbook (2006), originating from Hardy and Parfitt (1991).

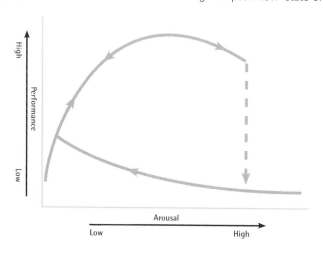

Where would you be on the arousal curve launching from this beach? Would it fill you with excitement or terror?

Self-confidence

We have all seen the overconfident sea paddler head into a cave on a big swell day and come out with their tail between their legs after a near miss (and perhaps a damaged boat). Conversely, out on a tidal race, we have seen the very talented paddler not prepared to give it a go due to a lack of confidence, despite it being clear to everyone else that they are more than good enough.

Self-belief is a key part of maximising performance and being able to cope when the going gets tough. To have the confidence to know what is truly possible is a real skill that is essential for the sea kayaker. For many of us, it is often low self-confidence that is holding us back and coping strategies need to be found for this. Overconfidence is a problem for some; this is often based on an unrealistic assessment of the situation and our ability to be able to deal with it. Overconfidence is a dangerous attribute and needs to be addressed.

Would you surf these waves? If so, would you be overconfident or self-confident? Getting it right is essential.

This chapter provides coping strategies for managing self-confidence, many of which are the same as arousal-coping strategies. For those challenged with low self-confidence, remember what the famous Jedi Master Yoda once said:

"THERE IS NO TRY, THERE IS ONLY DO..."

Attentional focus

When paddling in challenging conditions what is the main point of focus and what is the correct thing to be focusing on? Is your mind focusing on the big seas around and the things that could go wrong or is it focused on the feel of the boat, how connected you are to it and the strokes required for the sea immediately around you? When breaking into the flow is the focus on the rough water beyond the eddy line and where the rest of the group are, or is the focus on the eddy line and the specific skills to cross it effectively? How many times when rock hopping were you thinking "I must miss that rock, I must miss that rock, oops I've just hit that rock". Perhaps if the focus had been: "I am going to paddle through that gap, I am going to paddle through that gap", then the outcome may have been different.

With attentional focus we all have the ability to focus in a broad way (the big sea picture and what may happen) or in a narrow way (the specific skills required or the eddy line). At times we will need the focus to be broad and at times narrow; the trick is to realise what is required and not be distracted by the other. In addition to this, our attentional focus can be external (focusing

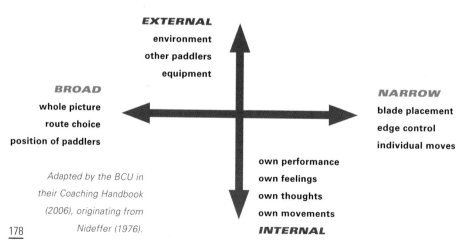

ATTENTION DIFFERENCE

EXTERNAL
environment
other paddlers
equipment

BROAD
whole picture
route choice
position of paddlers

NARROW
blade placement
edge control
individual moves

own performance
own feelings
own thoughts
own movements
INTERNAL

Adapted by the BCU in their Coaching Handbook (2006), originating from Nideffer (1976).

Before a trip I always make sure I get out and paddle as much as possible in rough conditions. My trip partner and I practise rescuing each other in tidal races and we'll paddle into waves and strong winds. This improves my fitness and skills but, most importantly, my confidence. I always perform better if I'm confident and the only way to get confident (rather than cocky!) is to get out there and practise in the conditions you are likely to encounter. You can't predict every eventuality on the water, but the more experience you have in different challenging situations then the better you will deal with whatever the weather and sea throw at you. A positive attitude helps, but knowing your own strengths and limitations is really valuable. I would advise going on trips to locations where you expect conditions that you are comfortable with. As your experience level increases, you can push yourself more (if you want to). There's no point in being scared senseless and risking your life. Be prepared!

Justine Curgenven

Justine has a peculiar habit of kayaking around things, including the South Island of New Zealand, Tasmania and the Queen Charlotte Islands. She makes award-winning DVDs, including the inspirational *This is the Sea* series and an instructional rolling DVD, *This is the Roll*. For more information, visit *www.cackletv.com*.

on the environment and other paddlers) or internal (focusing on our own feelings, thoughts and movements). There is a time and a place for both.

The same view with narrow and broad focus. Which would you need and can you switch between them? 179

Recognising the best point of focus prior to an activity helps to manage arousal and confidence; it prevents distractions and helps to keep things on track while performing.

Imagery

Imagery can be used in a variety of ways; when utilised as a key part of mental rehearsal, this is known as visualisation. Common uses for us as sea kayakers could be to manage arousal levels, build confidence, increase motivation, practise physical skills or rehearse tactics. Imagery is not imagining what could go wrong, but is the ability to develop clear pictures of performance in a structured way. It takes practise and training to be able to do this, but has been proven to be successful in many sports around the world. Read on for examples of how it can be used in sea kayaking.

Arousal management

If becoming over-aroused when about to break in to the flow, take a moment to focus on the skills required and slow the breathing down while doing this. Create an image in your head of you performing those skills in the perfect break-in; try to feel what is happening from your images as well as visualising your actions. Create this image with the sun shining; you are feeling confident and happy, maybe reflecting on a previous successful break-in. Use the positivity from the image to calm the arousal level. Similarly, this technique can also be used to help with self-confidence.

Using imagery to manage arousal and rehearse physical skills before surfing a wave on the tide race.

Physical skills

This time decide on the skill needing to be perfected (a sweep stroke perhaps). In the head, break down all the key parts of the sweep stroke and create an image of you performing them. Close the eyes to do this, add movements if it helps and try to see colours, hear sounds and feel emotions and movements. Perform the sweep stroke as an image in the head. Ensure that it is being done in real time and try seeing it as if you are actually doing it as well as looking down at yourself doing the stroke (i.e. an internal and external vision). This imagery can be practised just before performing the stroke while in the kayak, or at home in preparation for next time out. Either way, it will help to strengthen the knowledge and performance of the stroke.

Internal versus external imagery

Internal imagery is as if you are living the experience; it is how it is seen from the eyes of you, the performer. It is therefore important to make it as real as possible: feel the boat, paddle and water interactions, see the colours and hear the sounds. Often it will help to have the eyes closed. Allow the body to make movements as the image runs, making the image come to life. This internal imagery it is very powerful for skill acquisition.

External imagery is when you have a bird's eye view of what is going on, of you performing in a kayak down below. Making the image real is again important so that every detail of the perform-ance is captured, but this time you will be static and removed and the feelings of what is happening will not be there. It is as if you are watching a DVD of your performance. In this external imagery, there will be benefits from seeing the big picture tactics of what is required. It is also a great tool for self-confidence and motivation, for example visualising a previous successful performance prior to going out and trying it again.

Self-talk

Do you have a voice inside your head? Is this voice you talking to yourself? What do you say and does it help or does it hinder? Are we all going mad?

Believe it or not you are not going mad and yes, we all do it. The question is does this self-talk help or hinder us, and do we control what we say to ourselves. The uncontrollable self-talking that goes on in our head ('I can't do that', 'I am going to capsize', 'I wish I had not started', 'What am I doing here?') is known as negative self-talk. It is usually to the detriment of any performance and is more likely to confuse and clutter the head as opposed to help. This negative chatter in our head is incredibly powerful and not to be underestimated; we need to calm this chatter and ensure we can control the self-talk in our heads. What we need to replace it with is neutral or positive self-talk. When we are in control of the self-talk and are using it in a positive way, it will in time suppress the negative chatter; this can lead to good arousal management and increase self-confidence. We can use this self-talk to help perfect our paddling skills. There are two types of self-talk to consider, discussed in the following.

Positive self-talk

We all too often allow the negative self-talk to take over as a default setting. Positive self-talk is all about replacing any negative comments with a positive substitute, for example 'it is getting rougher, I might capsize' should be replaced with 'it is getting rougher, I have been in these conditions before and it was no problem'. The art of positive self-talk is to train yourself to use the positive version, or at least be aware that you have used a negative one and quickly change it. This style of self-talk is very good for managing arousal levels, helping with self-confidence and improving motivation.

Neutral self-talk

This is the kind of self-talk where there is no value given to anything in a positive or negative way; it is purely a statement of fact about what needs to be done. An example of this could be when breaking in: the self-talk in the head could be simply stating 'speed across the eddy line', or 'speed, sweep, brace when in the flow'. This type of self-talk is good for managing arousal as it provides a focus, but more importantly it is great for enforcing any key aspects of the skill that need to be remembered. The self-talk in the head could almost become the mantra for the skill, or the trigger words to help with timing and what needs to be done.

Planning and goal setting

When heading out on the sea on an expedition or day trip, there is only one way to prepare: plan, plan and then plan again. Think of all that may happen, and then do some more planning! If all feasible possibilities have been taken into account prior to an event, the paddler is always going to be in a far better place to deal with anything that may occur.

When it comes to managing arousal or developing self-confidence on the sea, do not wait until afloat: start by planning at home. By using this knowledge of what to expect and having thought through how to deal with the possible outcomes during the trip, arousal and confidence levels can be controlled. A plan is usually something that is put together not too long before a planned trip or expedition. That way it is fresh in the mind and can be part of the getting-ready process.

"FAILING TO PLAN IS PLANNING TO FAIL"

To help with your development into a confident rough water paddler (for example, undertaking expeditions or big open crossings), then your bigger plan should include some simple goal setting. Setting clear goals provides a focus, helps to monitor improvement and therefore leads to gradual success and increased self-confidence. All this helps with managing arousal and maintaining the optimum level through experience gained. Sea kayakers can break goal setting down into three main stages.

Dream goal

This is the final place you aspire to get to with your sea kayaking. For example, it could be to circumnavigate Ireland.

PERFORMER'S TOP TIP

Having the ability to make a good judgement is vital. Becoming confident in rough water is all about progression. A novice paddler would not and should not even contemplate paddling in a Force 8 wind and 3m seas. An expert might seek out such conditions, however, with the knowledge that depending on the direction of the wind, it's fetch and the intended route, paddling in such conditions can not only be relatively safe but also great fun. It's not about throwing yourself at the mercy of the sea.

A carefully considered judgement should be based on experience gained from progressively pushing one's limits in baby steps, under the guidance of those you trust to keep you safe. Always have an escape plan, and ensure that it does not rely on technology or the heroism of others. Confidence and ignorance are often confused in the inexperienced. Does good

judgement come from nurture or nature? Either way, it is the most important attribute of any rough water paddler.

Sean Morley

Sean circumnavigated the UK and all the inhabited islands in 2004. He is director of the Golden Gate Sea Kayak Symposium and an ACA Level 5 Instructor with California Canoe & Kayak.

Outcome goals

These will be some key outcomes that will need to be achieved prior to being ready for the dream goal. For the dream goal of circumnavigating Ireland, some outcome goals could be to improve tidal planning, become confident in rough water handling, get fit enough and efficient enough to paddle 40km days and develop on-the-water navigation.

Process goals

Having identified the main outcome goals that are required to achieve the dream goal, there needs to be a number of process goals in place to achieve each outcome. These process goals are often plentiful and need to be regularly reviewed and crossed off the list as they are achieved. They become the map of the journey that needs to take place to achieve the outcome goals. As the journey unfolds and they are reviewed, then changes will need to be made. It is during this journey that the plans already discussed will come into play.

When creating the plan for the process goals, ensure that the increase in challenge between tasks is set at a small step each time. If the challenge is increased in too-big steps, it could undermine self-confidence and result in failure. An example of this could be if you are wanting to surf on a tidal race when it is running on a spring tide. For this to be successful, the processes required could well include a solid roll in rough water, good kayak handling skills, tidal knowledge and a gradual progression of surfing from neap tides to eventually spring tides. Get the process in the right order and with the appropriate progressions and success will follow. Go surfing on the spring tide too early, and you could be put off surfing tidal races for life.

Example of goal setting

Specific

Measurable

Agreed

Realistic

Time Phased

Evaluated

Recorded

Consider a dream goal of having a 100% roll in tide races in two years' time. The process goal could therefore be to roll three times on each side every time you go paddling. The outcome goal could be to raise your success rate on flat water from the current 50% to 90% by mid summer; follow this by reviewing and re-setting the process and outcome goals.

For all of the goals above that make up the journey towards the dream goal, there is a simple rule which helps to decide whether a goal is a good one or not. It is called setting SMARTER goals.

Planning and goal-setting in sea kayaking is key for improvement, and will also help with confidence and arousal.

LAST WORD

You've read the book, studied the pictures and had plenty of top tips from some of the world's leading sea kayakers and coaches. Now it's time to get out there and put it all together!

I have enjoyed putting the book together and sharing my thoughts and experiences of paddling in the rough water environment. There is nothing more to add other than: get out paddling, have fun, learn lots and stay safe.

Happy paddling!
Doug Cooper

REFERENCES

Presentation at the Canoe England Coach Conference, Mark Woodhouse, January 2010.
BCU Coaching Handbook, Franco Ferrero (ed.), Pesda Press 2006, ISBN 0-954706161.
A catastrophe model of anxiety and performance, L Hardy and G Parfitt, British Journal of Psychology (82: 163–178), 1991.
Test of attentional and interpersonal style, RM Nideffer, Journal of Personality and Social Psychology (34: 394–404), 1976.

INDEX

Specialists in Sea Kayaks, Expedition Sea Kayaking, Courses and Paddles

SEAKAYAKINGUK.COM

Nigel Dennis
Designs

LENDAL

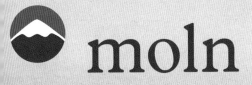

moln

Kayaking adventures

CROATIA	**GREENLAND**	**NORWAY**	**TURKEY**
FINLAND	**ICELAND**	**SCOTLAND**	**WALES**

www.moln.fi

Sea Kayaking Specialists - North Wales

Coastal Spirit

Coaching • **Guiding** • **Training**

Courses, expeditions & bespoke opportunities for individuals, families, groups & clu

t:01248 605056   m: 07873 13299
info@coastalspirit.com   www. coastalspirit.co

Rough Water Gear...

www.peakuk.co

t: +44 (0)115 9816622   e: info@peakuk.com   w: www.peakuk.co